'This book is a gem, beautiful in its look and feel, but more importantly, it is a powerful and accessible resource for developing your own mindfulness meditation practice and applying it to every aspect of your life—especially the most challenging and stressful dimensions. At the same time, it also reveals and guides you in practical ways to amplify the joy and wonder in simply being alive, and the invaluable, transformative, and healing power of fully inhabiting this moment in awareness.'

Jon Kabat-Zinn
Author, Professor emeritus of medicine and the creator of the 'Stress Reduction Clinic', and the 'Center for Mindfulness in Medicine, Health Care, and Society' at the University of Massachusetts Medical School

Calm the MONKEY Mind

A Scientific Approach to Mindful Living

DR MARTINA ESBERGER-CHOWDHURY

Hay House Publishers India
New Delhi • London • Sydney
Carlsbad, California • New York City

Hay House Publishers (India) Pvt. Ltd.
Muskaan Complex, Plot No.3, B-2 Vasant Kunj, New Delhi-110 070, India
Hay House Inc., PO Box 5100, Carlsbad, CA 92018-5100, USA
Hay House UK, Ltd., The Sixth Floor, Watson House, 54 Baker Street, W1U 7BU, UK
Hay House Australia Pty Ltd., 18/36 Ralph St., Alexandria NSW 2015, Australia

Email: contact@hayhouse.co.in
www.hayhouse.co.in

Copyright © Dr Martina Esberger-Chowdhury 2023

The views and opinions expressed in this book are the author's own and the facts are as reported by her. They have been verified to the extent possible, and the publishers are not in any way liable for the same.

All rights reserved. No part of this publication may be reproduced, by any mechanical, photographic, or electronic process, or in the form of a phonographic recording, nor may it be stored in a retrieval system, transmitted, or otherwise be copied for public or private use – other than for 'fair use' as brief quotations embodied in articles and reviews – without prior written permission of the publisher.

The author of this book does not dispense medical advice or prescribe the use of any technique as a form of treatment for physical, emotional, or medical problems without the advice of a physician, either directly or indirectly. The intent of the author is only to offer information of a general nature to help you in your quest for emotional, physical, and spiritual well-being. In the event you use any of the information in this book for yourself, the author and the publisher assume no responsibility for your actions.

Photo credits: Sandeep Solanki

ISBN 978-81-959917-5-4
ISBN 978-81-959917-4-7 (ebook)

Thomson Press India Limited, Faridabad, Haryana, India

To my late father, who started me on my journey home,
who lost, won, and lost again, only to realise
the unlosable.

Contents

Introduction   11
Preface   15

Part I
The Foundation of Contemporary Mindfulness

Chapter 1
What Is contemporary Mindfulness?   29

Chapter 2
Why Mindfulness Now?   45

Chapter 3
The Four Foundations of Mindfulness   55

Chapter 4
Managing Emotions with Awareness   77

Chapter 5
Compassion and Mindfulness   87

Chapter 6
The Science behind Mindfulness   101

Chapter 7
Benefits of Mindfulness and Meditation   111

Part II
All about Meditation

Chapter 8
The Art of Meditation   123

Chapter 9
Creating a Meditative Space　　　　　　　　　　139

Chapter 10
Meditative Postures　　　　　　　　　　　　　149

Chapter 11
Meditation Techniques　　　　　　　　　　　　157

Chapter 12
Breathing Exercises　　　　　　　　　　　　　169

Chapter 13
Common Obstacles in Meditation　　　　　　　181

Chapter 14
Living Mindfully　　　　　　　　　　　　　　193

Part III
A Selection of Meditations

Chapter 15
For Grounding　　　　　　　　　　　　　　　205

Chapter 16
For Focus and Clarity　　　　　　　　　　　　217

Chapter 17
For Resilience　　　　　　　　　　　　　　　231

Chapter 18
For an Open Heart　　　　　　　　　　　　　239

Chapter 19
For Giving and Taking　　　　　　　　　　　　249

Chapter 20
For Creativity and Innovative Thinking　　　　　257

Chapter 21
For Visualisation　　　　　　　　　　　　　　263

Chapter 22
For Gratitude　　　　　　　　　　　　　　　269

Chapter 23
For Just Sitting   275

Afterword   281
Author's Note   285
Acknowledgements   289
Bibliography   292
Notes and References   304

And you? When will you begin that long journey into yourself?
—*Rumi*

Introduction

This handbook is about the essence of contemporary Mindfulness, the science behind it, contemplations, and meditations that I have put together over the many years as a mindfulness and meditation teacher. Many meditations have become part of my daily practice and are integrated into my workshops.

This book aims to answer:

- What is behind these ancient practices and why is this universal approach more pertinent than ever in our disrupted times?
- How does the intersection of long-proven wisdom, psychology, and neurological science open insights into ourselves?
- What is self-knowledge and understanding?
- Why is it vital to reconnect with our bodies, thoughts, and emotions?
- What is the stimulus-response-reaction and how can we move beyond action on autopilot?
- What does presence have to do with success and relationships?
- Why should we observe our minds and the process of thought flow?
- What are primary and secondary suffering and how do we respond wisely?

- Why is our mind the key to understanding ourselves and how can we harness our minds to tap into our full inner potential?
- What is interconnection or interbeing?
- What does it mean to be content?
- What is the role of compassion and heart-wisdom in the science of living?
- What is my personal journey and the connection to these ancient practices?

Spattered between the chapters are quotations from religious and sacred poetry, prayer, and prose. Use these as an anchor to contemplate upon the words, write them in a journal, or memorise these passages of underlying and uplifting truth. This, too, is a form of meditation.

Audio recordings of some of the meditations described are available in English and German on my website: www.esberger-mindfulness.com.

May I be a guard to those who need protection,
A guide for those on the path,
A boat, a raft, a bridge for those who wish to cross the flood
May I be a lamp in the darkness
A resting place for the weary
A healing medicine for all who are sick
A vase of plenty, a tree of miracles
And for the boundless multitudes of living beings
May I bring sustenance and awakening
Enduring like the earth and sky
Until all beings are freed from sorrow
And all are awakened.

—The Bodhisattva Prayer, Shantideva

Preface

In June 1993, I was rudely awakened with a big bang from the infinite bright white tunnel of near-death, back into my body. Unbelieving that I was again in my physical body after two brain surgeries, I slowly worked myself back into the normalcy of life after a luminous near-death experience.

Whilst driving home, on a motorway in Vienna with the highest density of cars per day, after a busy day of work, I lost consciousness. My brain exploding inside, my head and shoulders fell onto the steering wheel, my foot seemingly disengaged from the gas pedal as the car veered from left to right, finally coming to a halt on the emergency lane. When I came to myself, I was in an ambulance surrounded by unknown faces, unclear about what had happened. 'I think I had an epileptic attack,' I fantasised in the haziness of half-sleep.

The neurologist at the emergency ward checked me thoroughly and I was allowed to be fetched by my husband after a few hours, with unclarity on the actual cause. There followed days of tests, magnetic resonance and CT scans, scintigraphy, blood analysis, and physician visits. The final report revealed an encapsulated tumour in my brain. It was situated in the right prefrontal cortex and was about a centimetre in diameter or the size of a hazelnut. Its growth had exerted pressure on the inner wall of the brain, leading to an electrical discharge which led to an epileptic fit. This had led to the near-fateful incident on the motorway. The diagnosis was clear, it was either a cancerous tumour of the brain or, if I was lucky, a benign growth. In the aftermath, it seemed as if a guardian angel had protected me on that spring day, as I drove home totally unprepared for the major upheavals ahead.

On the surface I was shattered. Deep inside was an acceptance of the diagnosis with composure. Soon, an open brain surgery was planned to remove the growth.

'A routine procedure, no problem in this era of medical expertise, nothing to be afraid of. Just walk into the hospital, you'll be on your feet the next day,' reassured the eminent Neurosurgeon.

On a hot June day, I checked into the tenth floor of the hospital with a stupendous view of the city skyline. The surgery was planned for the next day. My husband sat at my bedside until the late hours of the evening chatting about plans for our forthcoming holiday.

In the early hours of the next morning, a nurse arrived with a scissor and razor to remove my fringe and the hair on the front right-hand side of my head. She was encouraging about how hair grows back so quickly, but it was a shock to see myself in the mirror, white-faced, vulnerable, and clean-shaven. Shortly thereafter I was wheeled into the operating theatre with my partly bald head.

The operation was a success, I was told. The tumour thankfully emerged as being non-cancerous but was diagnosed as an encapsulated amoebic abscess. Amoebae are single-celled organisms that occur with greater likelihood in the tropics. Usually, they reside in the intestines and cause a sickness called 'amoebic dysentery' that responds very well to medication. Amoebae are often found in standing sweet water, ponds. or sometimes in swimming pools, and if they have an affinity to the host, they can wander up the nasal passages into the brain.

There, the amoebae live peacefully and without causing undue symptoms for a while, eventually enveloping themselves in a capsule. These organisms can lead to massive inflammation and meningoencephalitis, which can result in death. Not the pleasantest creatures.

I had been a champion swimmer in my school days, often spending every day in pools training. As captain of the school swimming team, I would participate in swimming meets quite often. This meant going to swimming pools in remote parts of Mumbai, where the quality of the water was not always perfect. It seems as if an amoeba had discovered my nasal passages and instead of wandering into my gut or into my liver, decided to find its path into my brain.

Without a detailed examination or CT scan and medication, I was released from the hospital within a week and sent home, somewhat shaky on my feet, but proclaimed medically fit. This would prove to be a fallacy.

During the first night at home, I fell into a coma during my sleep. The next morning, I did not wake up, instead I lay unresponsive in my bed.

There followed a race for my life. My mother, who had taken the day off to support me in my rehabilitation, and my husband, Alfred, took me to the hospital where a CT scan showed that a new tumour had developed in the right lower side of my brain, exerting considerable pressure on the brainstem. The tumour was the size of a walnut and was situated in that extremely sensitive part of the brain that's responsible for cardiovascular-respiratory-system control, pain sensitivity, alertness, awareness, and consciousness. The brainstem connects the rest of the body to the cerebellum. Injury could result in memory loss, speech impairment, difficulties in breathing and changes in personality. Grim prospects for a recently married thirty-five-year-old! Thus, an extremely tricky second operation with an unclear prognosis was scheduled.

I re-entered the same room on the tenth floor of the hospital, and within hours my skull was opened for a second time within a span of eight days. I had not an inkling of what had happened. My body lay immobile with gently closed eyes, my breathing was soft and regular, as if I were peacefully asleep. But what was happening within me, unseen for the outer world?

In my reality, the near-death experience into the world of bardo[1] had begun. I was floating in an endless tunnel of dazzling white light, gently being carried and caressed by intense love and compassion.

It was a silent and peaceful world into which I had floated. A bodyless, timeless, boundaryless, yet fully conscious entity—fully awake and aware of my surroundings. As if I was part of the vast ocean that constitutes life, of which we as sentient beings are the waves and ripples which come and go forever in the cycle of birth and death. The ocean as the creator and the created, the thinker and the thought, the breather and the breath. An ocean with the implicit energy, the rhythm of the universe pounding with the beat of the heart as it resonated in the now. Yet, no mind, no intellect, no body, no action, no reaction, no interaction, just the intense warm bath of selfless love and compassion. This world of in-between lovingly cradled me like a baby with selfless love, like in the womb of a cosmic mother. Had I come home to stay?

A sense of profound connection with my family prevailed as I watched them from outside my body, as they waited in deep sorrow, shock, and hope in front of the wake-up room of the operation theatre. Totally unaware that I had been released from pain and suffering and was entirely free and content. Compassion and warmth filled my being in this moment and the realisation that apart from transient memories there was nothing to grieve for.

The skilled hands of the neurosurgeon removed the second growth with great care. I was sucked back into the breathing body, lying in an intensive care bed with the lights and monitors around me beeping monotonously. Gently opening my eyes and readjusting to the glare of synthetic light, it took a while to fathom what had happened, so intense and real were my experiences in the afterlife. These memories have stayed with me for life, crystal clear, and always accessible. Impressions of the secret of life in all its subtleties, present simultaneously, open for us to see once the 'me' is dropped and the orthogon shifts.

The months thereafter left their scars, not just visibly on my skull and hairline but invisibly in fits of epilepsy occurring as my brain healed. A long stint in the hospital followed by a specific therapy for amoebiasis and a rehabilitation of a weak body. Relearning to walk, to speak, to focus, to hold my balance with baby steps and much patience with myself. At times it seemed as if the wound on the skull would not heal, and new complicated surgeries were required. This cup passed me by.

It took many months on that stony road back to normality. Months of relearning movement, self-confidence, speaking and clarity of thought, finding my way back in the slow process of recovery. These were months of introspection and a rebalancing towards purpose. Like the recalibration of an inner compass. My convalescence enabled the emergence of a connection to the fragility of life, the dawning of living fully in every moment and the sprouting of mindful experience. A deep sense of gratitude and humility arose for this precious gift, so often slept through.

Whilst I wobbled along, step by step, burning questions like, 'Would I be able to live a normal life?' flooded my mind. My physicians and psychologists did not seem to think so. 'Would I be physically or mentally impaired, possibly brain-damaged, chronically ill . . . On lifelong medication, unable to drive again, home-bound, dependant, and childless . . . ?'

I proved to myself and my family that it was possible to rise again after this death sentence. To heal, to rebuild the destroyed neurons (the neuroplasticity I will describe later in this book proven in action), and to slowly conquer and overcome my epileptic episodes. The worrying mind was pacified and trust in life, which takes care of life, awakened.

My late mother, my husband, and my sisters Nandita and Anu provided pillars of stability in times of ambivalence and uncertainty, for which I am deeply grateful. My father, who lived in Mumbai, shattered by my illness, motivated me again and again to believe in life. In the years that followed, I delivered a son, completed a PhD, and founded a social enterprise. As my self-confidence was restored, I re-entered the pharmaceutical industry to start on a second career, with much success.

Yet what is success? Is it a fantasy of the ego-obsessed mind whose existence itself could be challenged? The persona, I, me, and mine's results of doing? Again, essential questions pervaded my mind. Was the essence of that near-death channel of emptiness getting lost? What was the message from the forever pulsating field beyond space and time? What role did love and compassion play in this drama of life and near-death? How were emptiness and fullness part of the same game? This game of life? What was the role to be played in the unknown span of time gifted to me in this body?

The realisation that the human body is a gift, not to be irresponsibly wasted in the accumulation of material and other transient pleasures. The inner conviction that the years remaining were to be used to find the source, the secret, and purpose for existence. That the final merging of the micro-self with the macro-self was the only reason for my survival.

The clear understanding that the wheel of *samsara*[2], the cycle of birth, death, and rebirth had brought me into this body, in order to slowly dispel the veils behind which our true nature hides? In the words of the Persian Sufi mystic Rumi 'Knocking on a door. It opens. I've been knocking from the inside'.

What had emerged was a realisation that like in Plato's cave, the shadows are taken for reality and in believing in the three-dimensionality, their reality becomes my life. It is like becoming the actor, the plot and the set on a movie screen called living, with all the world a stage with many players. Each being has many roles to play until the curtain falls.

My childhood and young adulthood in India surfaced gently and prodded me subconsciously. The many years spent with my father, sitting in dimly lit auditoriums or on cricket lawns as the sun set across the Arabian sea, listening to different chapters of the Bhagavad Gita, rekindled a flame in the depths of my being. A slow evolutionary process of 'recognition' had begun, along with a return to the spiritual treasures of the country of my birth. The shift was an understanding through the heart-mind and not through the intellect, leading to the beginning of experiential inner knowledge. The journey from intellectual learning to heart-wisdom had begun.

The family I was born into had strong religious and spiritual roots. My Austrian mother's maternal uncle was one of the first supporters and followers of the anthroposophist Rudolf Steiner in the small town of Sankt Veit an der Glan in southern Austria. His sister, my grandmother, was steeped in the devotion of Catholicism. My father came from a lineage of Brahmin *zamindars* (landed gentry) from a border province to West Bengal, now in Bangladesh. The family had been scholars of religion and philosophy for twenty-seven generations and hailed from the Gangetic plains in Bihar, the seat of Indian wisdom and learning for centuries. My paternal grandmother was the daughter of a priest who had spent many years studying Tantric Buddhism in Tibet. My uncle, my father's youngest brother, had taken the vows of a *sannyasi* (monk) after a long career as a successful artist. Interestingly it was my mother's interest in Indian philosophy that had brought my parents together and triggered her voyage from the West to the East and her lifelong relationship with India.

My personal journey within had begun as a young girl. I had grown up in a cultured home in Bombay, as the megacity was called then, facing the Arabian sea. My parents were great art lovers, and our house was full of artefacts. Nestled between contemporary paintings were numerous antique statues of Buddha. The figures depicted the Awakened One in myriad forms—teaching, meditating, or standing with characteristic gestures or *mudras*. Some were hewn out of sandstone, others of white marble or black slate. My favourite image was a black granite figure of the Buddha Avalokiteshvara. Embodying compassion and radiating peace, it sat cross-legged in meditation. The quiet and thoughtful child that I was, I would gaze at the serene expression of the different sculptures in our living room for hours. Were Buddha's teachings of 'The four noble truths' being whispered in my ears and resonating from the images? Were these messages reawakening decades later?

My father was a passionate collector and supporter of modern paintings in the early sixties. Painted by now-famous artists of the time, some were abstract, subtle in colour, or depicted concepts of emptiness. Every few weeks, he would change the position of the paintings in the house or make place for a new piece. Then, usually on a Sunday afternoon, he would sit down in front of a painting and call us children to join him.

'What can you see in this picture?' he would ask. 'Look carefully, what is the painter traying to tell you? Just look. Become one with the image. With the colours. Nothing else. Sit and contemplate. Meditate . . . this is meditation.' His words have impacted me for life.

Apart from practising physical yoga or asanas regularly, I became a voracious reader of any Indian philosophical text I could lay my hands on. My first book on Vedanta was gifted to me by a family friend when I was barely fifteen. Called *Jnana Sudha* or 'Nectar of Knowledge', I remember devouring the book, perhaps without really understanding its true meaning. Thus started my exploration of the world of Vedanta, the philosophy of yoga, the Upanishads, Adi Shankara's *Vivekachudamani*, and the Bhagavad Gita to name a few. Later, this lay study was complemented with New Age thought from the west. Deep encounters with renowned yogic masters and the unfulfilled desire to become a nun, were further steps on my spiritual journey.

As the late Vietnamese monk, teacher, and peace activist Thich Nhat Hanh described eloquently, DNA or store consciousness arises as the body ages and hidden leanings from previous generations emanate and manifest. Perhaps this explains the paradigm shift in my destiny.

Decades later, in Europe, I embarked upon an intellectual reorientation, making my education and leadership experience redundant in the pharmaceutical sciences, marketing, and management as I plunged into the realm of mindfulness and meditation. The teachings of Jon Kabat-Zinn inspired me to step out of the corset of the strict yogic path I had been raised on and liberated me to a contemporary way of meditation, more suited to my life in the distracted, hectic west. My inner bearings shifted and that which had been intrinsically absorbed all my life evolved into reality. The 'I' was being turned inside out, the ego shattered, becoming a container for what was waiting to emerge.

Many retreats with different masters followed. I travelled to Germany, Portugal, and to the sacred city of Rishikesh on the banks of the still pristine Ganges in northern India. Rishikesh, home to masters since time immemorial, and to the Beatles, on their spiritual quest, resting at the foothills of the mighty Himalayan range. It always felt like I had returned home . . . sitting on the riverbank . . . listening to the rhythmic chanting of the *shlokas* or to the melodious songs to the gods, *kirtans*, and *bhajans* in the tiny shrines, echoing across the holy river.

My own spiritual path was slowly evolving to become a synthesis of the philosophic schools and experiential techniques that I had been exposed to. The merger of non-dualist teachings of Advaita Vedanta with elements from yoga, mindfulness, and the ethical and moral base of Buddhism gave me a steady rudder with which to steer through the still and stormy waters of life.

My initial forays into guiding short meditations culminated into teaching mindfulness in organisations and to individuals interested in the first steps of living mindfully. My personal lifelong search and my profession intertwined, leading to profound personal insights. My students have become my teachers, every word a reflection of my inner understanding. The container and the contained merge.

Resounding with the words of Sri Nisargadatta Maharaj, 'In the stillness of the mind, I saw myself as I am: unbound.'

Tuning into and staying awake with the underlying awareness which is the cause for all that we experience in a never-ending cycle of birth and death. A meditation that is the silent, effortless dance of life.

The one imperishable (letter) itself shines continually in the Heart. How is it to be written?

In the centre of the heart-cave Brahman alone shines in the form of the Self with immediacy as 'I-I'. Enter into the heart by diving deep, with the mind investigating itself, or with control of the movement of the breath and abide in the Self.

The body, like things made of clay, is insentient in nature and has no 'I'-concept. Also the existence of the Self is admitted at the time of sleep when there is non-existence of the body. Therefore, I am not the body. To those established as the Self and having seen with a sharp intellect adhering to the enquiry 'Who am I?' and From whence? Arunachala-Shiva itself shines full as the manifestation of I am that.

—*Muktaka Trayam*

Part I
The Foundation of Contemporary Mindfulness

Chapter 1

WHAT IS CONTEMPORARY MINDFULNESS?

Imagine walking along a familiar path every day—to the bus, to the car, to work, going shopping—with a destination in mind. You walk quickly. Suddenly, your world slows down like in a time machine. Each step is consciously felt in its intensity, every manifestation on the ground is perceived. The surface you walk on comes alive—hard, soft, cold, warm, yielding, firm, smooth, rough, and your feet develop sensors that capture the environment in its entirety just as it appears in this point in time. You hear the sounds around you, birdsong, the buzzing of the bees, the falling of the leaves as if in slow motion. You perceive a connection to the body, to all your five senses, your thoughts and emotions, and are fully present in the moment. Everything is seen as if from the eyes of a newborn baby, without judgments and preconceived opinions. You accept everything as it is. Maybe time has frozen? You have just witnessed a moment of mindfulness, a flash of awareness, perhaps experienced awe, and an instant of connection to the source of being.

Mindfulness is a state, a trait, and a training based on millennia-old wisdom that has its roots in contemplative traditions of the East. Buddhism, Hinduism, and Jainism from the Indian subcontinent; Daoism and Confucianism from China and the Far East; monotheism from the Middle East; and rationalism from Greece have contributed towards what is termed as mindfulness. In this book, I have used the words mindfulness and awareness interchangeably, as in my understanding both terms have the same meaning.

Described in detail in the Theravada Buddhist Pāli Canon, the *Satipatthana Sutta* and the *Mahasatipatthana Sutta* present discourses on the establishment of mindfulness. Satipatthana is a compound of *sati* (mindfulness) and either *patthana* (foundation) or *upatthana* (presence). The compound term can be interpreted as *sati-patthana* (foundation of mindfulness) or *sati-upatthana* (presence of mindfulness). These discourses stress the practice of mindfulness for the purification of beings, for the overcoming of sorrow and lamentation, for the extinguishing of suffering and grief, for walking on the path of truth, and for the realisation of nibbana, the release from rebirth.

Buddhist teachings originated in the north of India, present-day Nepal, over 2,600 years ago. It is said that the young prince Siddhartha Gautama, at birth, had received a prophecy that he would either be a great king or a great spiritual teacher. His father did not want him to become a monk, which led to him being brought up secluded within the palace grounds. One day he ventured with a servant to see the world outside the walls. The story goes that he encountered an ill man, an aged man, and saw a corpse lying by the wayside. He was deeply struck by these three forms of human suffering. The young man realised that these were the inevitable phases of life. On his way back to the palace, he was struck by a monk who embodied peace, stillness, and equanimity. Inspired, he decided to begin a path of inner discovery to understand suffering, its source, and how to end it. As predicted, Siddhartha Gautama became one of the greatest spiritual teachers who was named 'Buddha' or 'the awakened one' upon enlightenment. His orally imparted teachings form the basis of the world religion 'Buddhism'. Mindfulness, described in the next chapters, is an essential part of Buddha's teachings.

Mindfulness or awareness is simply about being conscious, awake, and alert at every moment of your life by deliberately paying attention to every instant, being fully engaged in whatever happens around and inside you, and bringing an attitude of interest, openness, curiosity, tolerance, and friendliness to whatever is encountered, rather than normal patterns of judgment and criticism. It is about not being overly reactive or overwhelmed by what is going on around us.

Many definitions of mindfulness exist. Jon Kabat-Zinn, one of the pioneers of the contemporary mindfulness movement in the west, defines mindfulness in the following way: 'Mindfulness is awareness that arises through paying attention, on purpose, in the present moment, non-judgementally.' Judging, in this context, means categorising something or someone into good, bad, or neutral and precludes grasping, disinterest, or aversion.

Mindfulness is a basic quality that every human being possesses. It is a question of learning ways to access it.

WHY MINDFULNESS?

The pace, complexity, and unpredictability of life have increased rapidly in recent years. A term coined by the military, known as VUCA—characterised by volatility, uncertainty, complexity, and ambiguity—describes our current reality. The unforeseen arrival of the Covid-19 crisis was an unprecedented example of how disruption can shut down the entire planet with all the consequences for society, human relationships, healthcare, and business, deeply challenging our understanding of life as it has been so far. Our social, economic, and political fabric is progressively faltering. War, climate change, migration, terrorism, violence, poverty, pandemics, and hunger dominate our world. We are destroying nature, our planet, and our lives. The impact of the effects of our lifestyles and never-ending consumption on our fragile climate system is threatening to play havoc with the environment. The fact that a normally animal-carried virus can jump to the human species is an indication for the dimensions of the disruptive times we live in.

Smartphones, laptops, tablets, and computers are our extended homes and offices, connecting us with our address books, calendars, notes, banks, schools, tickets, and everything we require with a swish of our fingertips. Our physical and emotional dependence on social media, chats, and blogs knows no bounds. While the Internet has connected us globally and allowed us unlimited opportunities to access information, conferences, and learning, the long-term impact of the digital revolution and artificial intelligence are yet unclear.

Added to this is the pressure that prevails in the professional world, permanent digital accessibility, and the increase in all forms of distraction, from internal and external sources.

We can hardly defend ourselves from distractions. According to a 2015 study by Microsoft Canada, our attention span is eight seconds lower than that of a goldfish. Scientific studies have shown that our minds wander for 47 per cent of the time. Medically termed 'Attention Deficit Trait' (Hallowell), our distracted minds lead to restlessness, emotional and physical exhaustion, aggression, and the feeling of being overwhelmed.

A mind that is constantly distracted cannot focus and think clearly, leading to stress, a rise in fear, despair, and worry.

Multitasking has become a characteristic of our times. Our brains are not built to perform different actions simultaneously, they are instead made to process one task after the other. Even though we are convinced that we are multitasking champions, the quality of whatever we do suffers immensely. We are drained of energy by constant switch times required by the brain to regenerate between moving from one task to the next.

Depression, burnout, and other mental illnesses are on the rise and have been labelled the scourges of our century, according to the WHO. Especially in the working environment, mental illnesses are the reason for absenteeism and long-term ailments.

The Covid-19 pandemic showed us the pitfalls of shutting down entire countries. Stretched healthcare systems unable to cope with the forecasted high rates of hospitalisation resulted in a stop of all cross-border travel and closing of all airports as global air travel ended. Except for life-sustaining professions, work was moved to home office, schools and universities resorted to homeschooling or online teaching, and traffic on the roads dropped to a minimum. Partly forced quarantine kept families at home, restricting contact with others, especially to people with a high-risk for the infection, the elderly, and chronically ill. The pandemic made entrepreneurship and businesses rethink their strategies for an uncertain and blurred future.

We are experiencing what Otto Scharmer, senior lecturer at MIT, calls the three divides: the social, the economic, and the spiritual. Today, in most social systems, we collectively produce results that nobody wants. These results appear in the form of economic, social, and cultural devastation. The ecological divide, which disconnects oneself from nature; the social divide, which disconnects one from another; and the spiritual divide, which disconnects oneself from oneself, shape a larger context in every major structure that is evolving today.

Mindfulness and a regular practice of meditation lets us build a relationship with ourselves and with others. To be fully awake in the moment, not in the past or in the future, where we are most of the time, but in the here and now. Perceiving the present moment in its fullness. Mindfulness strengthens the axis between body, emotions, and mind so that the sensory system is reactivated to an inner compass. Thus, the walking, standing, speaking, hearing, smelling, tasting, feeling in all their multidimensional facets come alive and the practice of mindfulness becomes an omnipresent part of living.

ASPECTS OF MINDFUL LIVING

An important aspect of mindful living is our attitude. Equally so are the attention and awareness we bring to our daily activities, sometimes called informal mindfulness. Being one in body and mind with what we are doing, be it a simple task of chopping vegetables or cooking, or a complex one of presiding over a meeting with important decision-makers, the secret is to be fully awake and present in the existing moment. Not in the yesterday, nor speculating about tomorrow, not mind-wandering or multitasking, but attending to whatever is arising now. A third component is that of active practise. Taking the time to ground yourself, to take a few conscious breaths, to connect to the sensations of the body, to watch your thoughts and emotions flow, and to respond compassionately if required. Apart from these three, how we deal with listening, empathy, emotional and social behaviour also constitute a part of an aware way of living. An ethical and moral value system forms the base of any spiritual practice. These rules on how we should live our lives are described in every religion, be it the Ten Commandments of the Old Testament, the eight Silas in Buddhism, or the *Yamas* and *Niyamas*—the ethical vows and morals of yoga in *Yoga Sutras of Patanjali*.

Jon Kabat-Zinn describes the following principles or attitudes of mindfulness: being non-judgmental, patient, having a beginner's mind, trusting, accepting, being able to let go/let be, and exercising non-striving. Other qualities of mindfulness that characterise our everyday life are kindness, gratitude, joy, and compassion. It is these attitudes that shape the way we behave, react, and live by embodying mindfulness.

A fundamental attitude is presence. Presence means being aware and fully awake in the current moment, with your mind, body, and all your senses. Presence goes beyond being just physically present in a conversation with people. It entails bringing our full attention to whatever we do, be it in interaction with others or whilst focusing on a task.

Because these principles are decisive, it is important to explain what is meant by them. Being non-judgmental involves attending to all that happens around us without immediately forming an opinion. Our experience is shaped by our thinking. However, our thoughts usually consist of past experiences and personal views, often coloured by prejudice, bias, upbringing, and social conditioning. We often unpack our preconceived ideas and project them onto the current situation. Through meditation, we learn to take a non-judgmental attitude towards everything that appears in the mind—an attitude of acceptance for what is emerging, be it a feeling, a sound, a thought, or a body sensation. We learn to do so without colouring it; labelling it as positive, negative, or neutral; or with a desire to grasp or reject what arises. Being non-judgmental is imperative when faced with an unknown situation that requires intuitive decision-making and when encountering someone unknown.

Seeing with a beginner's mind describes a way of perceiving things with openness and curiosity, as if looking at them with the eyes of a child. A beginner's mind is the opposite of being an expert. Seeing with a beginner's mind allows you to look at ordinary situations, people, things, or moments with a fresh and pristine look. A beginner's mind opens new perspectives, nurtures curiosity, lightness, freshness, and humour.

We are often in situations in life where we do not like what is happening to us. The Covid-19 shutdown is an example of an unavoidable circumstance that was unchangeable. Cultivating acceptance is to take things as they are. If something can be changed, then do your utmost to change it, otherwise accept it for the time being. Resistance triggers negative and stressful reactions, both in the body and in the mind. Studies have shown that resistance increases suffering as it multiplies the pain. Acceptance is by no means equivalent to passivity or apathy. It is an active choice that reinforces the intent to let things be as they are for the moment and live with them. The bigger picture is usually revealed when the dots are connected in hindsight.

There are many different definitions of the heart quality compassion depending on the context. Compassion arises when one turns towards suffering with the innate desire to alleviate it. Compassion can arise for oneself in the form of self-compassion (to alleviate self-suffering) or for others. Compassion is a personality trait that can be learned by practise. For compassion to arise, empathy to the pain or the suffering of the other is required along with the ability to slip into another's shoes. Compassion is offered unconditionally, not as an incentive for a reward or something to be gained. It has been described as the love of a mother for her child.

Patience reminds us that we, sometimes, must wait for the seeds of our actions to germinate. Things often do not happen immediately, and patience is an attitude that gives us the gentle tenacity and courage to sit it out, be it pain, discomfort, unpleasantness, or eagerness for a result. This applies to meditation and to life in general. Just like grass that is tugged at will not grow faster, similarly every reaction has its own timeline to fructify and is not necessarily linear. Sitting out lies at the heart of success.

Trusting in yourself, your body, and your emotions are essential to mindfulness and meditation training. Learning to have conviction and faith in your intuition, expertise and self-knowledge let you trust in yourself. Act with the intent that the fruit of action lies not in your hand, is a verse often quoted from the Bhagavad Gita.

WHAT IS THE CONTEXT OF NON-STRIVING WITH MINDFULNESS?

Jon Kabat-Zinn describes non-striving in his book *Full Catastrophe Living* as follows: 'Meditation's only goal is for you to be yourself. The irony is that you already are. This craziness may be pointing you toward a new way of seeing yourself, one in which you are trying less and being more. If you think, "I am going to get relaxed, control my pain, or become a better person," you have introduced an idea in your mind of where you should be, and that you are not okay right now. This attitude undermines mindfulness, which involves simply paying attention to whatever is happening.'

As we begin to pay attention to our inner experience, we quickly discover that there are certain thoughts, feelings, patterns, and circumstances that the mind seems to want to hang on to. Likewise, there are others that we're trying to get rid of or want to stop to protect ourselves. In mindfulness, we let our experience be as it is. Letting go is a way of letting things be as they are, without wanting more or rejecting, without liking or disliking.

Transience reminds us that nothing is permanent. We want things to stay as they are forever, but if we look closely, we see that everything is impermanent. The seasons of nature, passing through the yearly cycle of awakening, blooming, ripening, and decaying, the caprioles of the weather, political systems, the ageing of our own bodies from the second we are born, and everything we encounter has a limited lifetime. As the mind-clock ticks, we realise how transient every moment is. Consciously being present in the current moment, by connecting to our bodies and to the experienced, allows the current moment to be enjoyed in its fullness moment by moment.

These principles flow into each other like an infinity circle, each causing and affecting the other. When we realise the inner meaning of each attitude, we bring the words to life and discover the connection to ourselves and to one another.

Just as in Buddhist and Jain texts, the texts of Patanjali refer to moral codes *yama* and self-restraints *niyama*, which are the starting points in these systems. Patanjali divides his system of yoga (Raja yoga) into eight steps, of which moral codes and self-restraint are the first two. Thereafter he mentions *asana* (movement) and *pranayama* (breath), followed by *pratyahara* (sense withdrawal), *dharana* (concentration), *dhyana* (meditation), and *samadhi* (union).

But what are these codes and conducts? Patanjali describes truth, non-violence, celibacy, non-stealing, non-aggrandisement, external and internal purity, and contentment. Self-discipline and self-control require a certain quality of mind, which grows upon you as you practise meditation regularly.

Mindfulness exercises our brain to be more consciously aware of what happens as it occurs, allowing us to turn towards experiencing with curiosity and presence and to take in every facet of experience. It cultivates the awareness of our thoughts, feelings, and body sensations and their interactions.

The slowing down and bringing our awareness to our senses allows us to encounter and value the richness of life, especially in the ordinary, often overlooked aspects in our surroundings. Mindfulness opens a sense of awe and wonder in us, in that it hones the power of perception, allowing us to fully engage with our senses and sense organs.

In exercising mindfulness, the thoughts are witnessed simply as thoughts, which is as a result of the mind's activity. The same goes for emotions. Seeing an emotion as just an 'emotion' of fear' and not 'my fear' or 'a feeling of anger' or not 'my anger' helps us free ourselves from clinging to our emotional states or feelings. We create a larger picture (what, why, when, etc.), recognise the reasons, and react through a differentiated and cause-related analysis. Mindfulness results in a closer relationship with the body, allowing us the perception of emotions arising before they are labelled by the mind. This leads to us become more intuitive towards ourselves and fine-tuning our emotional intelligence. Although we cannot control what arrives in our life, we can control how we react to it. Mindfulness does just that.

A saying claimed by several traditions' states:

Watch out for your thoughts, for they become words.

Pay attention to your words, for they become actions.

Pay attention to your actions because they become habits.

Pay attention to your habits because they become your character.

Pay attention to your character because it will be your destiny.

DEFAULT MODE VS PRESENCE

Research studies show that when we are not deliberately paying attention to something, our brain moves into default mode. The default mode is characterised by mind wandering, which often results in ruminating about the past or worrying about the future, negative thoughts, and operating on the so-called autopilot. Sometimes this is referred to as 'mindlessness'. In this busy, hyper-connected world, we tend to lose ourselves often in the autopilot mode . . . just 'doing' and constantly ticking off things on our never-ending to-do lists without really living.

When in default mode-specific areas of the brain—mostly in the temporal and parietal lobes—along with the hippocampus and certain prefrontal areas are activated. The amygdala, the fight, flight, and freeze centre of the brain, is overactivated. This pattern of activation tends to result in the world being experienced through thoughts and ideas (secondary paths) rather than via the senses (primary paths). Hence, increasing the chances of mental health problems such as stress, anxiety, and depression. Studies have shown that the default mode is also associated with reduced cognitive functioning, leading to reduced academic and occupational functioning. It has also been linked to difficulty in understanding others and communicating effectively.

Being mindful is the opposite of mindlessness. We take over the steering wheel of our attention and pay deliberate attention to what we are doing. This mode of functioning engages different areas of the brain, primarily located in the prefrontal regions such as the insula and the anterior cingulate cortex.

When we move out of the default or autopilot mode, we maintain a moment-by-moment awareness of bodily sensations, our thoughts and our feelings, and the surrounding environment. We experience things directly through our sense organs and avoid getting caught up in all the aspects of an often-unhappy mind on autopilot. This state of being is experienced when we are effortlessly in the present moment and at one with what we are doing, be it playing an instrument, spending time with the family and friends, doing a sport, or just being in nature.

THE BIGGER PICTURE

Mindfulness begins with learning to focus on the current moment. Ultimately, it becomes about connecting with the awareness that is conscious of whatever we experience— the awareness that tastes with the tongue, feels through your skin, or hears with our ears at this moment.

Focusing on the breath in the moment gently improves our attention skills. Once we can focus our attention, we can start to differentiate between what we are aware of in each moment and what it is that is aware. Connecting to this awareness, allows us to realise that the awareness itself stays permanently unchanged, whereas what it is aware of is impermanent and changes from moment to moment. Furthermore, like a big movie screen or the sky, awareness or consciousness—or whatever you would prefer to call it—has the inherent quality of openness and acceptance to whatever is occurring, remaining still and calm in the background.

The great Sufi mystic Rumi is quoted: 'Remember the door to the sanctuary is inside you' and 'They say there is a doorway from heart to heart, but what is the use of a door when there are no walls?' Nisargadatta Maharaj, the renowned Advaita master, in his book *I Am That* said: 'The inner and the outer are part of a never-ending dance of life, always here simultaneously, forever present, beyond the concepts of form, time and space.'

As we live in the here, in doing mode and rest in the being mode within, letting happen, leaving the 'I' or persona, the role we play on the surface is non-attached. The essence of living fully in the river or flow of life, moving from one fully experienced and wakeful moment to the next, active in non-reactivity.

Bringing an open and accepting awareness to ourselves and others, we become kinder and more compassionate, transforming the way we interact and relate to one another. As our ability to sense this clear, open awareness grows with practise, our equanimity and emotional balance remain constantly present in any situation. The practice of mindfulness meditation allows us to gain insight into our true nature and into the essence of being.

Once you realise that the road is the goal and that you are always on the road, not to reach a goal, but to enjoy its beauty and its wisdom, life ceases to be a task and becomes natural and simple, in itself an ecstasy.
—*Sri Nisargadatta Maharaj*

Chapter 2

Why Mindfulness Now?

*H*ave you ever thought about the nature of your mind? Is your mind identical to your brain? Could it be situated elsewhere in the body . . . in the vast nerve centres in the heart, or in the gut, or in the heart or gut brain? Where do we locate that which knows that which remembers our skills, or that by which we learn?

Various studies show that we have between 60,000 to 80,000 thoughts a day. On the one hand, the ability to think and apply our intellect has enabled humankind to evolve and move us from the caveman to a civilisation at the dawn of the industrial revolution 4.0. On the other, war, destruction of nature, strife, hatred, greed, and power are threatening the very core of our civilisation. These, too, are created by the human mind. Our minds and intellects can create both heaven and hell, invention and destruction.

Negative thoughts have the quality of being sticky, like Velcro, according to neuroscientist Rick Hanson. This has evolutionary reasons, as any threat could have been a life-ending experience. As negative thoughts collect, they can lead to a downward rumination spiral. On the other hand, positive thoughts do not leave a lasting impression on the brain and, therefore, must be consistently reinforced. Rick Hanson describes this phenomenon of the brain as being like Teflon, positivity flows away like oil from a non-stick pan. Techniques such as journalling, positive affirmations, noting good things that happen during the day, altruism, or simple gratitude are ways we can foster positivity. Being aware of these characteristics of our thoughts help us decide on what we entertain.

When we sit still and begin to focus on the breath, we notice how noisy our minds truly are. But once we become familiar with the practice of breathing meditation, we find that the mind produces thoughts by itself and that us and our thoughts are not identical. Thoughts simply take place. Thoughts are just mental processes and not absolute truths. These thoughts, which take the shape of plans, judgments, opinions, assessments of our perceptions, or disjointed arisings, distract us from the observation of the flow of breath. We see that the thought process is not subject to any laws. We flit from the past, brooding over events that cannot be changed, to projecting things into the future that have not yet occurred. In the cultures of the East, the busy mental process is called the 'monkey mind'. Perhaps you can picture your thoughts swinging like a monkey from branch to branch and from tree to tree, never coming to rest. The manifestation of thoughts is the purpose of the mind just as sensations arise in the body.

Thoughts affect your feelings, body sensations, and behaviour, and the more you can distance yourself from your thought flow, the more effective and life-changing this simple exercise is. By getting lost in our thoughts, often generating fantasy castles, we forget about the present moment by losing connection to the here and now, which is the only moment we have. Just recognising that your attention has been hijacked and returning it gently but firmly on the breath or onto your current activity is an act of recognition and mindfulness.

There are many ways in which defusing can help address distracting thoughts. For some, it helps to see a thought as a soap bubble floating away in the wind. You can visualise thoughts as clouds passing by on the vast, clear, luminous sky, which remains unaffected. Or imagine your mind like a cooking pot that is simmering. With every thought bubble that comes up and bursts, the thought dissolves. The mind is often depicted as a never-ending train with countless carriages. Imagine yourself as standing on a bridge above and watching the train as it moves by, not stepping into a carriage, and allowing the train to pass by, wagon by wagon. This is learning to remain as an observer and focusing on what we are attending to.

Do you know that there are different ways of knowing and being in the world? The conceptual and experiential modes of the mind allow us to experience the world. Conceptual thinking is the practice of connecting abstract, disparate ideas to deepen understanding, create new ideas, and reflect on past decisions to plan for the future. The conceptual mind can understand abstract concepts—like the function of a complicated business or a non-linear digital process—easily. The conceptual mode is called the 'doing' mode.

Experiential or being mode involves direct experience in the present moment, with all our senses.

Our minds are constantly being flooded by diverse thoughts and depending on our mode, we provoke a certain atmosphere or colouring. If we observe carefully, we will notice that our minds keep shifting. Sometimes we are in automatic mode or habitual ways of thought and behaviour, other times we are in present-moment awareness. Conceptual and experiential modes switch back and forth. By training our attention we can observe the content and workings of the process of the mind from moment to moment, which allows us to choose the direction in which we intentionally move our attention. This broadens our awareness about the nature of thought and the power of the mind.

By pausing again and again during the day, we can bring our mind to experiential mode and allow a rejuvenation of the brain—by listening, taking in smells, awareness of taste, touch, visual impressions, and just being with them.

See thoughts as a mental process that appear in your mind and do not necessarily correspond to the absolute truth. Create a distance between yourself and your thoughts. Do not allow feelings or emotions to waylay you. Observe, accept, and let go.

Tips to Observe the Mental Process

- Bring your awareness to your thoughts
- Observe positive and negative thoughts, attachment, rejection, or neutrality
- Take a step back from your thought flow

ATTENTION AS THE ENTRY POINT FOR EXPERIENCE

Why is attention so vital in this world full of noise and distraction? According to psychologist and philosopher William James (1890), attention is 'the taking possession by the mind in clear and vivid form, of one out of what seem several simultaneously possible objects or trains of thought.' Over 130 years ago James described the phenomenon that what you focus on becomes your reality.

Attention is the ability to focus selectively on a selected stimulus, sustaining that focus and shifting it at will. This suggests that you selectively 'attend' to a single mental thought, and it is this thought that goes forward in the mind. However, attention is far more than this. Attention is often used interchangeably with the ability to concentrate. However, these are not the same. A different way of thinking about attentional focus is like the beam of a spotlight used to pick up pertinent information in a similar way to a police helicopter searching for suspects at night. You are flexible in where you 'direct the beam'.

Concentration, on the other hand, is about being totally immersed in the here and now. The past and future are not important. Your focus on the present seems effortless. A few elements are key to concentration. These are the ability to focus selectively, to maintain focus over a period of time, to be fully aware of what is unfolding around you, and to be able to alter attentional focus as required.

Many publications have appeared around the different forms of attention and the importance of attention for performance.

Herbert Simon, a Nobel Laureate in Economics, warned in 1997 that living in the information era results in a lack of attention. Not only do we have to deal with frequent mental and sensory distractions, but we also have to cope with an onslaught of technology that leaves us with little time to reflect. This often makes it difficult to focus, especially when we need to complete tasks such as reading for meaning, thinking deeply, or communicating carefully. As Daniel Goleman says, we can often 'hopscotch' or 'multitask', which negatively affects our capacity to excel in whatever we do.

The ability to multitask was for a long time considered an important asset in organisations. However recent studies have shown that the brain can only focus on one task at a time and needs to complete one activity to begin with the next one. Try writing a line of numbers and letters of a simple sentence like 'I can multitask' alternatively. You will be surprised at your stress levels. Multitasking leads to an exhaustion of the brain, mistakes, and fatigue.

Knowing we are working on multiple tasks one at a time is the first step in being able to bring our focus to just one activity. Completing one task and then moving on to the next one ensures that our attention is not pulled back and forth.

A well-known experiment, 'Gorilla Test' by Simon and Chabris (1999), demonstrated the uncanny power of single-pointedness. It shows how the mind prioritises what is demanded of it and thereby fails to register what is occurring outside of this window of perception. People are shown a short video of two teams passing basketballs. One team is dressed in white, one in black. The viewers are instructed to count the number of passes made by the team in white and ignore the number of passes made by the team in black. Halfway through the film a person in a gorilla suit appears in the video, thumps his chest, and walks out. His appearance lasts approximately nine seconds. Most people who watched this video did not see the gorilla and cannot believe that one appeared. Although the eyes register the person in a gorilla suit, the viewers are so focused on counting the number of passes that their minds do not actively take in the disturbance. A simple experiment that demonstrates how our attention is the gateway to experience.

THE STIMULUS-RESPONSE MODEL

You may recognise the following situation. You are driving and suddenly a car cuts in from the wrong side. You brake instantly, with a glance in the rear-view mirror as your anger rises.

'Can't you wait?' you shout, honking loudly and gesticulating wildly. A common incident on the streets of a big city.

Each stimulus provokes a response. You may ask what a stimulus is? A stimulus can be described as everything we can potentially perceive in the external or internal world. In the external world these can be light or sound. In the internal world these are body sensations and sense impressions that our minds can differentiate and name. Examples are feelings of itching, tension, temperature, moisture, or pain. Our autopilot mode ensures that vital reactions happen mechanically. In the background, below the visible iceberg, unconscious behaviour patterns, emotions, and preferences control us without us being aware of them. It is known that 96 per cent of our decisions are subconsciously made. These ingrained behaviour patterns are sometimes triggered by experiences which can be traced back to childhood, which we are most often unaware of.

The practice of mindfulness allows us to consciously become aware of valid stimuli, pause for a moment before reacting, and then respond. In this moment of awareness, we can decide more freely and independently how we want to react and respond, leading to conscious decision-making. Thus, we reduce the impulsiveness of the default mode.

The survivor of the Holocaust and Austrian psychiatrist Dr Viktor E. Frankl summarised this life-changing realisation in this quote often attributed to him: 'Between stimulus and response lies a space. In that space lie our freedom and power to choose a response. In our response lies our growth and our happiness.'

We have the power to choose our response to our circumstances and thus to shape the outcome; indeed, we have the responsibility, and if we ignore this space, this freedom, the essence of our life, our legacy could be ignored. This gap allows us to take a step back, to stop short and distance ourselves for an instant, so that we can react wisely.

The practice of mindfulness lets us build a strong relationship with our thoughts, feelings, and body sensations. As we cultivate this ability, we intuitively make conscious and aware decisions to meet the challenges of everyday life and eruptive behaviour becomes a thing of the past. Instead of reacting on autopilot—based on ingrained habits—we choose to respond skilfully with wisdom and clarity. Past traumas arising are gently met by the breath and are allowed to heal in this space of compassion.

What could be an alternative ending to the story of the car and driver? I drive calmly in the car, fully aware of the traffic and pedestrians around me. I choose not to be distracted by a driver who rudely edges himself in. Who knows the reason for his rashness? Perhaps an ill child or mother? An emergency? Pain or death? Instead, I greet the driver with a compassionate smile, remain equanimous, present, awake, and conscious of all that is occurring.

The fool thinks, 'I am the body'; the intelligent man thinks, 'I am an individual soul united with the body.' But the wise man, in the greatness of his knowledge and spiritual discrimination, sees the Self as the only reality, and thinks, 'I am Brahman'.
—***Adi Shankararcharya***

Chapter 3
THE FOUR FOUNDATIONS OF MINDFULNESS

One of the most moving texts that has deeply influenced my understanding of mindfulness is the Satipatthana Sutta, briefly mentioned earlier in this book as a foundation of mindfulness. Over 2,600 years old, the Satipatthana discourse provides a practical map for establishing mindfulness in every aspect of daily living. There are numerous translations and interpretations available. Bhikkhu Analayo's books *Direct Path* and *Satipatthana Meditation: A Practice Guide* and Joseph Goldstein's book *Mindfulness: A Practical Guide to Awakening* are excellent guides.

The Satipatthana Sutta forms the basis of mindfulness practice. It describes the four foundations of mindfulness as:

1. Mindfulness of the body (i.e., breathing, the experience of the body, anatomical parts, postures, degenerating corpse, activities)
2. Mindfulness of feeling (the appraisal of experiences as pleasant, unpleasant, or neutral leading to grasping or aversion)
3. Mindfulness of the mind and mood (experience or absence of mind states)

4. Mindfulness of our experience of the world (i.e., five types of *dhammas* for contemplation, the mental hindrances, the aggregates, the sense spheres, the awakening factors, and the four noble truths)

These four foundations of mindfulness are interactive elements of experience that inform and form each other. All the elements that are required for true transformation lie within our human body, the mind, feelings, and our worldly experiences. We have everything within us to deepen our understanding of ourselves and the universe.

Mindfulness training cultivates all these elements as part of experiential practice. The first verse of the Satipatthana Sutta introduces the four Satipatthana or foundations of mindfulness as the 'direct path' to realisation and begins:

Thus have I heard.

At one time the Blessed One was living in the Kurus, at Kammasadamma, a market-town of the Kuru people.

Then the Blessed One addressed the bhikkhus as follows: 'This is the only way, O bhikkhus, for the purification of beings, for the overcoming of sorrow and lamentation, for the destruction of suffering and grief, for reaching the right path, for the attainment of Nibbana, namely, the Four Arousings of Mindfulness.'

The Buddha goes on to explain the four arousings of mindfulness and provides a brief description of each one (*Satipatthana: The Direct Path to Realization* by Analayo).

What are the four? Here, monks, in regard to the body a monk abides contemplating the body, diligent, clearly knowing, and mindful, free from desires and discontent in regard to the world. In regard to feelings he abides contemplating feelings, diligent, clearly knowing, and mindful, free from desires and discontent in regard to the world. In regard to the mind, he abides contemplating the mind, diligent, clearly knowing, and mindful, free from desires and discontent in regard to the world. In regard to dhammas he abides contemplating dhammas, diligent, clearly knowing, and mindful, free from desires and discontent in regard to the world'.

The mental characteristics required for this path are repeated after every element and an integral part of the direct path to nibbana. They are diligence or the application of effort (*atapi*), the presence of clearly knowing (*sampajañña*), and a mindful state of mind that is free from desires and discontent.

Sati or mindfulness represents the deliberate cultivation and improvement of the receptive awareness in the initial stages of the process of perception. Important aspects are an alert, open state of mind and equanimous receptivity. The de-automation of conditioned responses and perceptual assessments is one of the core tasks of sati. Mindfulness leads to a gradual restructuring of perceptual appraisal and climaxes in an undistorted vision of reality 'as it is'. An important element is being actively non-reactive, by neither suppressing nor instinctively reacting to the content of our experience, a so-called middle path.

The 'refrain', which emphasises important aspects of the practice is repeated thirteen times in the Satipatthana Sutta following every verse. The refrain describes the arising and passing away of internal and external phenomena and emphasises that mindfulness leads to an awareness than is unbroken. The clarity obtained is independent of grasping, clinging, or adhering to.

FIRST FOUNDATION OF MINDFULNESS: THE BODY

The basis for experiential learning in mindfulness practice is the cultivation of mindfulness of the body. Whether we sit, stand, walk, or lie down, we learn to become aware of the body as the body. A body that is always in the present moment as it cannot be in the past or the future.

Especially in our times of extreme body consciousness, many of us have a paradoxical and superficial relationship with our bodies. We overidentify with the physical aspects of shape, weight, beauty, skin colour, age and dictates of the fast-changing fashion world to name a few discriminatory factors. The body usually appears on our radar in the face of discomfort or pain and body regions suddenly get magnified when in distress. We often react with resistance and repeated questioning, thereby increasing our pain even further. Usually, moments of extreme pleasure or physical pain bring our attention to truly feeling the body, instead of a continuously flowing awareness of what is. Mindfulness practice allows us to release a life in our minds and emotions to focus on whatever is arising in the body as we are sitting, standing, lying down, or moving.

The Satipatthana Sutta begins with the contemplation of the body, whereby the breath is seen as an elemental part thereof.

The practice of mindfulness-based stress reduction (MBSR) uses an exercise called the 'body scan', which takes the meditator on a journey through the body, whilst focusing the attention on the sensations arising during the scan. This is usually carried out in the lying-down position, we focus our attention and awareness on our mind on each region in the body, mostly beginning with the left foot and feel and are aware of whatever sensations are present in that moment. The MBSR body scan moves from the left leg to the right leg, then via the hip girdle upwards to the lower and upper abdomen, the chest, the spine, and shoulder blades. Moving through the arms, the attention is brought to the left and right hand and finally via the neck to the face and the crown of the head. The meditation concludes with a focus on the breath and the awareness of the flow of the in-and-out breath as we breath naturally, connecting to the present moment by this lifelong process of breathing.

The body scan or body sweeping practices are akin to relaxation techniques used for the body by Jacobson or the tantric Yoga Nidra. Their focus varies from deep relaxation to tapping into the individual parts of the body in a certain sequence to generate a deeper connection with the body.

In his book *Coming to Your Senses*, Jon Kabat-Zinn describes over thirty physical sensations, often dual in nature—such as warm/cool, dull/sharp, or light/heavy—that can be encountered during a body scan. He speaks of emotional reactions that may occur like impatience or wanting to stop, enjoyment or wanting to continue, boredom, sadness, fear, or anger. Thought processes that can be observed are reviewing the past, speculating about the future, planning, evaluating, analysing, going around in thought-circles, judging, labelling, or comparing your current experience to past ones to name a few.

The body scan is not for everybody, and it is not always the meditation of choice even for those who love it. 'If you think of your body as a musical instrument, the body scan is a way of tuning it. If you think of it as a universe, the body scan is a way to come to know it,' says Kabat-Zinn.

Mindfulness of the body can lead to a deepening relationship with our bodies, the elements, the changing nature of life, and the insights of the essence of inhabiting this framework of human existence. Being embodied in life, this practice uses our bodies as a vehicle for the discovery of the larger aspects of being. A functioning body is key to be able to practice any spiritual path; thus, sickness or an aversion to the body can become an obstacle towards liberation.

A mindful connection with our bodies can lead to numerous insights, beginning with the knowledge of the body as the *body* and seeing sensation as *sensation*. Below are a few insights that have been observed in the course of an inquiry into the experience of a body scan. Practitioners are requested to share their experience verbally in a group, usually directly after the scan is over. Sometimes insights, pleasant or unpleasant, occurrences or feelings are written in a journal, especially when a body scan is practiced for a week at a stretch. I have also used structured questionnaires as a mode of feedback. These observations provide the meditator with a deep understanding for this body-based practice, fostering body-awareness, sensibility, and connection.

Sometimes the body scan can evoke a greater intensity of sensations in the body. Sensations are often perceived with less judgement and positive or negative reactivity. Pain can occasionally be felt more intensely and often results in our observing the sensation of pain more closely. Is it permanent or does it wax and wane? Does the intensity vary moment by moment? What role do our thoughts and emotions play in the process? Is the memory of pain and fear greater than the actual sensation of pain?

What happens when I lean into or befriend my pain or discomfort? Does it soften and allow the tenseness to slowly dissolve?

The body scan enables us to create an idea of distance between the sensation and awareness, allowing a greater intimacy with bare sensation, opening to the give-and-take between the sensations themselves, and our awareness of them. This leads to being less disturbed by them or relating to them in a different way. Attending with awareness teaches us to let them be as they are and to hold them without triggering emotional and mental response. It is as if the sensory feeling of the experience is unhinged from the emotional and cognitive dimensions, which sometimes leads to a reduction in the intensity of the sensations experienced.

We learn to see the body as the body with the whole spectrum of sensations that occur from moment to moment. The pleasant, the unpleasant, the neutral are accepted as they are, bereft of judgement, delving into cause and reason, anxiety, and the emotional roller coaster that drives us into worry, distress, and speculation.

The relationship that is cultivated with the body enables us to feel emotions somatically, thus, being able to react implicitly before the mind checks in. This is of great importance when dealing with triggers of stress as a mindful body is a warning system. An example would be someone who is afraid of cats. The presence of a cat causes the heart to beat faster, a classic fight-or-flight response triggered by the amygdala, the fear centre in the brain. The body reacts before the arising emotion of fear is processed by the brain and then by thought processes and reactions, like running away or freezing in fright. It is the sense of fear that enables us to react differently and, perhaps, be with the cause of stress, the cat, in a natural way.

We become aware of the interconnected nature of the body and the mind, each affecting the other. In joy our bodies feel light, at peace, and wide open. Whereas in pain we feel tightness, tension, narrowness, and are closed off.

A fascinating aspect of mindfully discovering the body is the ways in which deeply rooted patterns and traumas slowly emerge and/or release. By attending to certain areas of the body wherein these patterns are lodged with kindness, we can resolve long carried burdens. This leads to a letting go of the old traumas and pain. The breath acts as a gentle, friendly way to dissolve the ingrained.

A skill that is trained by the body scan is not to allow one's attention to be distracted by thoughts, images, plans, or judgements, which usually occur during the practice. Letting all distractions pass by, like clouds in the sky, and returning to the region of the body that we are attending to, strengthens our ability of concentration and focus. We learn not to react impulsively and enter a thought train, a faculty we can always apply in our lives.

Holding the body with friendliness, care, and compassion with the message: 'I care for you; you are a part of me,' and not with aggression, anger, resentment, or resistance open pathways to healing from within. Visualising breathing with love for your own body helps regenerate your injured cells. Imagining the transport of oxygen and nutrients to the afflicted area sooths the hurt and pain from within. Just as we can soothe the body, we can awaken self-compassion for deeply rooted negative judgemental tendencies. By assuring ourselves that these are a part of the human condition, they eventually dissolve and melt away.

Mindful motion with full awareness of the body and breath enables our focus to detach itself from outer distractions and reside wholly inside the body. Our bearing and posture radiate our ability to stay grounded. When we sit, we are sitting, when we lie down, we are lying down, when we stand, we are standing, when we walk, we are walk in tune with our bodies.

The role of the body appears in several important ancient texts of yogic literature—Sage Patanjali's *Yoga Sutras*, *The Hatha Yoga Pradipika* by Swami Swatmarama, *Goraksha Samhita* by Yogi Gorakhnath, *The Gheranda Samhita* by the mystic Gheranda, and a text known as *Hatharatnavali* by Srinivasa Bhatta Mahayogendra were written between the 6th and the 15th Centuries AD.

Yoga of the body or Hatha yoga combines two root mantras or syllables representing the vital force (*ha*) and the mind or mental energy (*tha*). Hatha Yoga causes the union of both forces to take place, leading to the awakening of higher consciousness. The objective of Hatha yoga is to create an absolute balance of the interactive processes and activities of the physical body, mind, and energy, thereby purifying the body.

According to the masters of Hatha yoga, the first discipline is related to the body. The subtle elements (*tattvas*), the energy channels (*nadis*), the vital force (*prana*), the entire nervous system and various secretions in the body should be maintained and harmonised to be able to practise sense withdrawal and meditation. Thus, Hatha yoga or mindfulness of the body is described as the preliminary practice of mindfulness.

In discovering the first foundation of mindfulness, namely the body, we consciously become aware of our breath and our experience of it. Our breath is our companion from the instant of our birth till we take our last breath. Observing the breath in all its facets and learning to be mindful of the breathing process leads to focus, concentration, and peace in stressful situations. An awareness of the breath, whether it is slow or fast, shallow or deep shows us how interconnected we are with the body state. When we are calm, our breath is regular, slow, and deep. When agitated or under stress, the breath becomes fast, shallow, and sometimes irregular. Thus, a close observation of the breath lets us know our experience somatically. The Satipatthana Sutta describes the breathing process incorporated when we focus on the breath. Known as *shamatha* or concentration meditation, it seeks to bring about peace and tranquillity.

By observing our breath, we realise that everything is constantly changing, that all sensations arise and pass, and that we are just spectators. We learn that our bodies are not fixed, but fluid, and our thoughts, emotions, and experiences are transient. Our minds create thoughts just as our bodies allow sensations to arise, from moment to moment. These insights can lead to less identification with the body and what it represents.

In the eight-week MBSR programme, we encounter a number of ways to establish mindfulness of the body. Examples are:

- Body scan practice
- Mindful movement practices
- Sitting practice
- Walking practice
- Mindfulness of eating
- Three-step breathing space practice

SECOND FOUNDATION OF MINDFULNESS: THE FEELING TONE VEDANA

The second foundation of mindfulness deals with the emotional evaluation of an object as a primary experience.

Every impression on the senses has an emotional tone that is perceived as pleasant, unpleasant, or neutral which is neither pleasant nor unpleasant. Pleasant and unpleasant sounds, smells, sights, tastes, touch, physical sensations, and thoughts are all part of our everyday experience. Everything we perceive is implicitly connected to the tone of feeling and we react depending on whether we find it pleasant or unpleasant. Certain experiences are universal, such as the reaction to hunger or pain, but many reactions are subjective and related to things like our culture, upbringing, preferences, etc.

The emotional tone begins as soon as an experience unfolds. It is like a trigger, because if reactivity is suffocated at the core, it cannot arise.

Why is it so important to deal with the tone of feelings? The feeling—which is described as pleasant or unpleasant or neither pleasant nor unpleasant—gives rise to cognitive processes in the mind, which in turn lead to emotional and physical reactions.

Thus, pleasant sensations can cause overwhelming surges of desire, grasping and greed, which in turn lead to actions. Sensations perceived as unpleasant can provoke rejection and aversion, which also lead to emotional and cognitive patterns.

Mindfulness supports us in perceiving the feeling tone from moment to moment. We learn to perceive the pleasant as pleasant and the unpleasant as unpleasant, freeing ourselves from all sorts of further reactions that arise from speculation, identification, and habit. We become aware of how sensations and experiences can be transformed by the tone of feeling in the direction of desire (affection) and aversion (rejection) and trigger stuck patterns. All this happens in the present and influences the future. Mindfulness reveals these processes and allows us to be freed from them.

As important as the 'tone of feeling' is for the feeling in the present moment, we must not confuse it with emotions. Emotions are far more complex and arise later in the process of sensation. The tone of feeling is quite simple, the first moment of contact and the sensation that results from it in the context of pleasant, unpleasant, or neutral. There are two ways of looking at the neutral feelings described in the Salayatanavibhanga Sutta. There are those associated with ignorance and those with wisdom. They are related to whether such feelings transcend their object. When in ignorance or confusion, neutral feeling is predominantly the result of the bland features of the object where the lack of effect on the observer results in the absence of pleasant or unpleasant feelings. Neutral feelings related to the presence of wisdom transcend the object since they result from detachment and equanimity and not from the pleasant or unpleasant features of the object.

The verse on feeling tone in the Satipatthana Sutta says:

> This frame of reference correlates with a link in the twelve-fold chain of dependent co-arising (between feeling (*vedana*) and craving (*tanha*), thereby presenting an opportunity to intervene in the cycle of suffering.
>
> Exercises such as the three-step breathing space (see page Nos. 172-175) give us the opportunity to perceive the feeling tone.

THIRD FOUNDATION OF MINDFULNESS: THE MIND AND OUR MOODS

The third foundation of mindfulness is a deeper awareness of our current state of mind and mood. This includes the spectrum of basic emotions such as satisfaction, awe, and envy. Positive mental moods such as joy, love, or gratitude are experienced. Many of these states of mind involve complex compositions of thoughts, feelings, and body sensations and have different forms of expression. Each emotion has different facets and can cause different behaviour.

There are subtle differences between cultures suggesting that our state of mind is shaped by our upbringing and cultural context. Some examples of attitudes are:

- Basic emotions such as happiness, sadness, fear, anger, amazement, disgust, shame, and arrogance
- More complex emotions such as joy, love, gratitude, recognition, interest, embarrassment, worry, depression, fatigue, boredom, schadenfreude, exhaustion, and resentment
- Attitudes such as consistency, calm, sharp, distracted, dull or constricted, peaceful and agitated

Mental sensitivities, especially negative emotional states, can be compared to a tinted lens through which we view the world. The colour of the lens creates a subjective picture of our experiences. Moods cause an attention bias that prevents us from being fully present in every moment with an open mind and without any judgment.

Mental states lead to trains of thought and narratives that reinforce them, thereby pouring more oil into the fire. A mood of sadness rarely leads to thoughts of possibility or happiness. A single sensory experience can trigger a mental state, which in turn can release pathways of perception that nourish that state. It's a vicious circle. If we observe our mental moods closely, we will find that difficult, negative moods lead to long, often obsessive, and captivating storytelling. Mental states of contentment, happiness, or peace are less associated with narratives or ruminations but are expanding and flowing. They strengthen our potential to deal with challenges.

In my courses, I stress the role we have in dealing with the management of our mind, thought processes, feelings, and emotions. Whether I choose to follow the negative—often the result of long-established set patterns—or make a conscious decision to pursue the positive, the steering wheel lies in my own hands. The awareness of these mechanisms is, for many, the first encounter with the role of the mind and the way our experiences are coloured by the moment. Our autopilot mode and ingrained habits obscure our vision and the chance to be there in the present moment.

With the increased sensitivity to perceiving our body sensations, we gradually learn to feel emotions in the body. Especially when dealing with stress, it is important to realise a sensation arising in the body as soon it occurs. The pause before a fixed mental or emotional reaction allows a recognition of the effects of the stress sensation, and, thus, stop it at its source before it can harm the body or the emotional system.

With the practice of mindfulness, we learn to perceive the spectrum of mental states and moods in a distinguished way. We begin to understand which mental sensitivities have positive effects and which have negative effects. By observing ourselves closely, we remain fully aware and conscious of the emotion and thought process arising without acting rashly. In doing so, we deliberately take a different path that prevents suffering, dissatisfaction, and pain. The strengthening of a helpful state of the mind allows us to cultivate the good and the positive, thereby promoting healing. It helps with difficult mental states to bring attention back to the body or to feel the flow of breath. In this way, we deliberately interrupt the train of thought and minimise the negative effects.

Mindfulness teaches us to recognise feelings under the premise of 'being there'. Instead of feeling 'I am sad', disassociate to feel 'Sadness is here' or 'Fear is here'. We slowly become familiar with a vocabulary that describes our mental state. A thought is a thought, a mood is recognised as such, feelings and emotions are perceived as they are—as passengers, not facts. 'Thoughts are just thoughts,' writes Jon Kabat-Zinn. By detaching ourselves from identifying with them, they lose their power over us. Mindfulness allows an understanding of the changeability of our mental states and sensitivities so that we can perceive both the good and difficult moments, especially the moments of contentment, happiness, awe, and appreciation.

Practices from the MBSR programme, such as the three-point breathing space or the listening meditation, allow us to consciously perceive our mental and emotional sensitivities.

FOURTH FOUNDATION OF MINDFULNESS: THE DHAMMAS

This stage integrates the previous three stages leading to an observation of the totality of physical and mental processes. This final stage is equivalent to becoming aware of the five aggregates, form, feeling, perception, formations, and consciousness so that one's world is seen as consisting in the interplay of five groups of physical and mental processes. Dhammas include processes and events that constitute sentient experience, and in this sense one's 'world', continually arising and passing away in relationship with each other and subject to multiple causes and conditions.

The word *'dhamma'* (in Pāli, 'Dharma' in Sanskrit) has been interpreted in many ways. The Sanskrit word *dharma* originally meant the 'law of nature' or 'the truth'. Dharma (*dhāretīti dhammam*) was a term used in ancient India to describe that which is ingested and lived by. The dharma of the mind was defined as that which arises on the surface of the mind at a given moment. The mind imbibes nothing other than its own nature and traits, which are its dharma. Dharma referred to the features and nature of a specific element. Dharma was also known as *rit*, the law of nature. For example, it is the nature of fire to burn everything it encounters. Similarly, the nature of ice is to be cold, and it cools whatever it touches.

Dhāretīti dhammam is the dharma that which is experienced and imbibed. Knowledge as lived experience allows us to become truly dharmic in life. If we live with fire we will certainly burn; if we touch ice, we will remain cool. This phenomenon cannot be altered. This, again, is *rit*, the universal law that governs all without exception and it does not differentiate between people belonging to different religions, communities, or countries. It is nature's law that all sentient beings will have to go through the cycle of birth, illness, old age, and death. This law is dhamma.

If we examine the nature of the mind, we will discover that emotions and thoughts such as anger, animosity, jealousy, or arrogance arise. These negative emotions have been called the nature of the mind, i.e., the dharma of the mind. Any negative emotion that arises causes a great agitation within. This is its nature. It is inevitable. When anger arises, another part of nature—namely agitation—

will follow inevitably. The misery arises with its own consequence or effect every time it does.

In his book *Sattipatthana: The Direct Path to Realization*, Analayo speaks of 'categories of phenomena', which underline the different functions of the elements of experience. It describes the following basic principles of the Buddha's teachings:

the obstacles,

the groups of existence,

the aggregates,

the sensory realms,

the awakening factors, and

the four noble truths.

The fourth foundation of mindfulness shows us how to implement these truths, these dhammas, independently in daily life.

In *Mindfulness: Ancient Wisdom Meets Modern Psychology* by Willem Kuyken and Christina Feldman, the five reaction pathways that trigger mental suffering mentioned in the sutta above. These are the five hindrances.

We long for things to be different and desperately try to replace the unpleasant with the pleasant. The mind reacts to the difficult, challenging, and unknown with unpleasant experiences to eliminate, suppress, dissociate, or avoid them. As soon as we cannot avoid or get rid of something difficult, restlessness returns, and we begin to ponder as we seek ways to judge the world of circumstances and the experience of the moment.

When a solution to the problem is impossible, we dissociate from it as a way to distance ourselves from the reality of the moment. Through all these recognisable patterns run doubt—doubt about the capacity to change us or our aspirations to live the life we long for. These doubts and scepticism can direct themselves against us.

In hindsight, we tend to forget ourselves, which undermines intentions, aspirations, and mindfulness, so that we mindlessly forget to consciously perceive our experience with a beginner's mind and with kind attention.

The practice of mindfulness makes us aware of how these habitual patterns arise and influence our behaviour. We recognise that these patterns (also concerning stress) are mental states and that habits that can be changed, especially with the knowledge of the neuroplasticity of our brains. Sustainable resilience, compassion, and well-being develop from within these patterns. They cannot be formed from outside.

The four noble truths the Buddha spoke of are central and universal, irrespective of time and space and are the essence of Buddhism. A fundamental element of the fourth foundation of mindfulness is a verse contemplating mental objects in the mental objects of the four noble truths, described in the following words: 'This is suffering according to reality; he knows, "This is the origin of suffering," according to reality; He knows "This is the cessation of suffering," according to reality; He knows, "This is the road leading to the cessation of suffering," according to reality.'

The first truth identifies the innate physical and psychological pain, or the innate misery, pain, and suffering intertwined in the essence of life; the second truth classifies the origin and cause of the pain; the third truth recognises the state in which the pain and its cause cease, thus it is absent; and the fourth truth formulates a course of practice toward this state.

The method known as the 'Eightfold Path' charts the methods by which the end of suffering is attained. These steps are Right Understanding, Right Thought, Right Speech, Right Action, Right Livelihood, Right Effort, Right Mindfulness, and Right Concentration.

As the meditator contemplates the world of dhammas, the mind eventually settles in a state of concentration that involves an initial direct seeing of the four truths.

Thus, the direct path to freedom described in the verses of the Satipatthana Sutta guide us through contemplations that open up aspects of subjective experience becoming more and more subtle as the discourse proceeds. Important elements that are required are continuous effort or *sadhana* (practice), a mind in equilibrium, unaffected by desire and discontent and the clarity of knowledge, seeing things as they are. Mindfulness is at the centre, driving these three components.

***

Whenever I visit the holy city of Rishikesh in the northern foothills of the Himalayas, I walk along the banks and ghats of the Ganges. Inevitably, I pass a ghat where Hindus traditionally burn their dead. The corpse bound in a white sheet and placed on a bamboo stretcher is usually carried down the steps to the river on the shoulders of the male relatives. Garlands and flowers cover the body on its last journey. After the rites of passage by the priest, the funeral pyre of wood, twigs, and sometimes sandalwood is traditionally ignited by the eldest son. The ashes are collected thereafter and handed over to the relatives in a sealed earthenware pot. This pot or the ashes are then poured into the river in a separate ritual. Often this takes place at dawn when the sun is rising over the waters. The ashes are accompanied by little baskets made of fig leaves, filled with orange marigolds and tiny candles, which float downstream until they, too, disappear—a symbol of transience. Women were not allowed to participate in a cremation until recently. This should shield them and allow them to mourn the deceased in the privacy of their homes amongst other women in the family.

It is considered auspicious to perform the last rites near the Ganges and immerse the ashes into the holy river. Many princely families had palaces or mansions in cities like Varanasi where they spent the last days of their lives. Since time immemorial it is believed that the water of the Ganges helps to free the soul from the cycle of birth and death.

A verse on transience in the Satipatthana Sutta, which touched me deeply, is the detailed description of the degeneration of a corpse. Also known as '*Asubha*' (foulness or unattractiveness of the body) or the contemplation of the ten stages in the process of decomposition of a corpse. The aim of this verse is the elimination of attachment and desire for the body, as this, too, is impermanent.

The verses portray the sight of a corpse thrown in a charnel ground in vivid colours and with gory details on the process of decomposition. Even today burning sites are populated by birds like vultures or hawks who prey on dead animals. The verse on impermanence proceeds to illustrate a skeleton and its disconnected bones, 'bleached white, the colour of shells', bones rotten and crumbling to dust and likens it to the current body, which goes from dust to dust. Being of the same nature, it cannot escape this fate.

Remembering the stories my father had told me about *sadhus* (ascetics or holy men) who spent days and nights near cremation grounds to gain insights about the transitory nature of human existence, these verses echoed within me, whilst I watched unknown bodies being consumed by the flames, until there was nothing left but dust. Impermanence and interdependence as part of the story of life, constantly repeating itself for eons of time.

Out of the soil of friendliness grows the beautiful bloom of compassion, watered with the tears of empathic joy, under the cool shade of the tree of equanimity.
—**Longchenpa**

Chapter 4
MANAGING EMOTIONS WITH AWARENESS

*B*ecoming aware of our emotions unwraps a new facet of how we deal with not only ourselves but others as well. Feelings are mental experiences of body states, which arise as the brain interprets emotions—themselves physical states—arising from the body's response to external stimuli. The order of such events is: Feeling threatened, experiencing fear, and then wanting to fight, freeze, or flee. This mechanism of response is deeply ingrained in our DNA as we have evolved from hunters and gatherers to a sedentary mode of living.

Emotions, like thoughts, come and go as currents and arise in the body before we can register or interpret them in our mind. Our storytelling mind usually adds some heaviness and leads to an experience of discomfort in addition to the combination of feelings and body sensations. We have our ways of dealing with difficult emotions like anger, disgust, or fear. And these tend to be habitual to divert our attention or subdue whatever is occurring in the present moment. It is helpful if we can look at the reasons behind a certain emotion that's arising because this is where we can access mindfulness. Dealing with our emotions and sensations mindfully, allows us to cultivate a changed connection to whatever is showing itself.

Were you aware that feelings such as love, hate, joy, and anger that occur due to a certain stimulus usually do not remain in the body for very long? Take an emotion like hate. Hatred, like all automatic reactions, lasts only ninety seconds from the moment it was triggered to the moment it subsides. Usually, we allow the storytelling mind to add fuel to the fire after an emotion arises, which causes the feeling to last much longer. So, if an emotion lasts longer than ninety seconds—which is usually the case—it's because we decided to rekindle it.

According to American author and neuroanatomist Dr Jill Bolte Taylor, who published these findings, your emotion should only last one and a half minutes. To experience an emotion, we need to have a thought, which triggers an emotional cycle in our brain. This, in turn, creates a physiological response in our body. In a recent study researchers examined twenty-seven different emotions and collected insights into the average time each emotion persists. Grief lasts the longest of all emotions—an average of 120 hours.

In her groundbreaking book, *My Stroke of Insight*, Dr Jill B. Taylor explains, 'One of the biggest lessons I learned was how to feel the physical component of emotions. . . . I could feel new emotions flowing through me and then release me . . . that I have the power to choose whether I want to hook into a feeling and prolong its presence in my body or just let it flow out of me quickly. When a person has a reaction to something around them, there is a 90-second chemical process that takes place in the body. After that, any remaining emotional response is triggered by the person who chooses to stay in that emotional and physiological loop.'

When something happens in the outside world, biochemicals are flushed through your body, putting it in alarm mode. These chemicals take less than ninety seconds to disappear from your body. This means that you can watch the process for ninety seconds, you can feel it whilst it is occurring, and then you can observe it dissolve. Your thoughts, either by choice or by default, stimulate whether you stay in the loop and prolong the process.

How can we stop this process? We can relax into the emotion and wait for ninety seconds until the feeling has disappeared. Whilst the biochemical process is switched on, we should be open and receptive for whatever is occurring. Usually, we react in a contrary fashion. We start a whole lot of thought processes and end up getting the body and mind to run away from the feeling instead of letting it pass. By training to be present, as mindfulness teaches us, we can counteract this reaction.

My experience in working with difficult emotions shows that simple exercises help in dealing with them. They often help to:

- Acknowledge the emotion arising and focusing your compassionate, welcoming attention on it, dropping the story associated with it. Just be with the emotion for some time, allowing yourself to experience it directly and in its totality. Do not judge the emotion or classify it in any way. Where in your body do you experience the emotion? Is it constant or does it change or transform itself. Try to remember with what sensation this emotion arises, so that in future the body can act as a radar before it emerges.
- Ground yourself. Feel the floor—the texture of the carpet and the tiles or the ground on which you are sitting. This helps to bring your attention

out of your head and into the ground. If you feel comfortable, take two or three deep breaths and stimulate your parasympathetic nervous system until you feel calmer and more relaxed.

Emotions show up in the way our bodies express themselves. For example, when we are afraid, our eyes are wide open and our eyebrows are raised. We may shout or scream in fright and breathe heavily and frequently. Most languages have idioms that describe the bodily sensations. Fear is often experienced as a 'shiver down your spine', you are 'scared stiff', or you 'shake like a leaf'.

A group of scientists in Finland have been studying the correlation between bodily sensations and emotions. In a paper published in 2013, they described a heat map where different emotions manifest in the body. In repeated experiments the results were the same. 701 participants were shown two silhouettes—one for positive and one for negative emotions—alongside emotional words, stories, movies, or facial expressions. They were asked to colour the bodily regions whose activity they felt to be increasing or decreasing while viewing each stimulus. Negative emotions like sorrow, fear, or anger caused sensations of coldness, especially in the lower extremities of the body. Positive emotions such as pleasure, love, or happiness were located in the upper parts of the body and associated with a feeling of warmth. Samples across Western Europe and East Asia showed similarities, suggesting that the link between emotions and the body is not culturally different, but a universal phenomenon.

Subjective feelings are a central feature of human life. In a further study on emotions, published in 2018, research scientists defined the organisation and causes of a virtual feeling space involving 100 core feelings that ranged from cognitive and emotional processes to somatic sensations and common illnesses. The feeling space was determined by a combination of basic dimension rating, similarity mapping, bodily sensation mapping, and neuroimaging meta-analysis.

A total of 1,026 participants took part in online surveys. Organisation of the feeling space was best explained by basic dimensions of emotions, mental experiences, and bodily sensations. Subjectively felt similarity of feelings was associated with basic feeling dimensions and the topography of the corresponding bodily sensations. These findings revealed a map of subjective feelings that are categorical and emotional.

The stronger relationship with the body cultivated by mindfulness, mindful movement, and meditation induces an immediate experiencing of an emotion when it arises. Through practise the emotion is dealt with at the source, through recognition of the sensation that is arising correlating it to the event it was triggered by, and then allowing and observing the feeling that occurs. Mindfulness makes us aware of our emotions head-on, like a mirror allows you to see yourself, revealing what needs to be addressed. The effect is the disbandment of, sometimes, long-term emotional patterns like anger, fear, or disgust.

In her book *Radical Compassion: Learning to Love Yourself and Your World with the Practice of RAIN*, American psychologist and mindfulness teacher Tara Brach describes a meditation to deal with difficult emotions. The acronym 'RAIN' stands for Recognise, Allow, Investigate, and Nurture:

1. **Recognise what is happening** by consciously acknowledging, in any given moment, the

thoughts, feelings, and behaviours that are affecting you.

2. ***Allow the experience to be there*** just as it is; you might recognise fear and allow it by whispering to yourself, 'It's okay' or 'this belongs' or 'yes', creating a pause that makes it possible to deepen attention.

3. ***Investigate with interest and care***, call on your natural curiosity—the desire to know the truth—and direct more focused attention to your present experience and felt sense in the body.

    You might ask yourself: What wants attention the most? How am I experiencing this in my body? What am I believing? What does this vulnerable place want from me? What does it need?

4. ***Nurture with self-compassion.*** Try to sense what the wounded place inside you needs the most, and then offer some kind of gesture of active care that might address this need. Does it need a message of reassurance or forgiveness or love? Experiment and see which intentional gesture of kindness helps the most to comfort, soften, or open your heart. It might be the mental whisper, '*I'm here with you. I'm sorry, and I love you. And I'm listening. It's not your fault.*'

AFTER THE 'RAIN'

When the active steps of RAIN are completed, it is important to notice the quality of your own presence and rest in that wakeful, tender space of awareness.

Welcome all the emotions, sensations, and feelings as the Sufi poet, philosopher, and mystic Rumi writes in one of his most famous poems 'The Guest House':

> This being is a guest house.
> Every morning a new arrival.
> A joy, a depression, a meanness,
> some momentary awareness comes
> as an unexpected visitor.
> Welcome and entertain them all!
> Even if they are a crowd of sorrows,
> who violently sweep your house
> empty of all its furniture, still,
> treat each guest honourably.
> He may be clearing you out
> for some new delight.
> The dark thought, the shame, the malice,
> meet them at the door laughing
> and invite them in.
> Be grateful for whoever comes
> because each has been sent
> as a guide from beyond.

A PARABLE OF ARROWS

A famous parable of the two arrows illustrates clearly how we magnify distress by not recognising the first arrow of sorrow but by compounding suffering and adding on further reactions, thus drowning ourselves in a volley of self-created arrows.

The Buddha asked a student once: 'If a human being is hit by an arrow, is it painful? Is it even more painful if the individual is hit by a second arrow?' Then he went on to say: 'In life, the first arrow cannot always be influenced by us.' The second arrow is our answer to the first. And with the second arrow arises the possibility to choose our reaction.'

Taken from the Sallatha Sutta, the story goes on to describe the teaching:

> The Blessed One said, 'When touched with a feeling of pain, the uninstructed run-of-the-mill person grieves and laments, beats his breast, and becomes distraught. So, he feels two pains—physical and mental. Just as if they were to shoot a man with an arrow and, right afterward, were to shoot him with another one so that he would feel the pains of two arrows, in the same way, when touched with a feeling of pain, the uninstructed run-of-the-mill person grieves and laments, beats his breast, and becomes distraught. So, he feels two pains, physical and mental.'

In the years of the pandemic, we all witnessed the first arrow due to the emergence of the Coronavirus. We were affected by restrictions on travel, on social distancing, on quarantine and lockdown, on curbs when meeting the elderly, eating out, working remotely, homeschooling, having to wear masks, and adhering to a strict hygiene regime.

But the volley of second arrows, our anxiety about getting infected by the virus or the worry that someone in our family may get infected, long-term financial implications, loss of employment, and the constant sensational news of the spread of the virus and numbers etc., which fill our newsfeed in all media, are avoidable.

In a nutshell, the first arrow, inevitably, causes pain but our resistance to it provides the ground for the second arrows. This is natural as our body, mind, and emotions react to a crisis.

The sutta then explains how it is possible to avoid the second arrow:

> Now, the well-instructed disciple of the noble ones, when touched with a feeling of pain, does not grieve or lament, does not beat his breast or become distraught. So, he feels one pain—physical, not mental. Just as if they were to shoot a man with an arrow and, right afterward, did not shoot him with another one, so that he would feel the pain of only one arrow, in the same way, when touched with a feeling of pain, the well-instructed disciple of the noble ones does not grieve or lament, does not beat his breast or become distraught. He feels one pain—physical, and not mental.

What does this story tell us? Sorrow, stress, or pain (the first arrow) are part of life. Combining the pain with resistance, worry, fear, clinging, craving, or avoidance (the second arrow fabricated by the reactivity of our mind) is our own choice; thus, it is avoidable. Our secondary suffering is often much more burdensome than the primary suffering, sometimes smothering us and obscuring all possibility of release, as distress is cumulated and extended. By mindfully becoming aware of all the emotions and thought streams that arise, we can change the way we relate to our experience, taking full charge of our lives. We interrupt the cycle of conditioned behaviour and distinguish between the two arrows.

A clear understanding of our mind, the thought flow process, the role of emotions and feelings, and their correlation with body sensation allow us to steady our boat in choppy waters and steer it with confidence.

We are what we think.
All that we are arises with our thoughts.
With our thoughts we make the world.
Speak or act with an impure mind
And trouble will follow you
As the wheel follows the ox that draws the cart.

We are what we think.
All that we are arises with our thoughts.
With our thoughts we make the world.
Speak or act with a pure mind
And happiness will follow you
As your shadow, unshakable.

—**Anonymous**

Chapter 5
COMPASSION AND MINDFULNESS

Contemplative traditions have recognised the benefits of compassion for centuries. In the last decade, research into the effects of compassion has shown that it has the capacity to promote prosocial behaviour[3]. In addition, psychological and physiological impacts have shown that compassion meditations have an impact on mental health treatment, making this ancient practice relevant as a complementary therapy.

The four qualities of friendliness, compassion, empathetic joy, and equanimity are also known as the four 'Immeasurables'. They are also mentioned in all great religions of the Indian subcontinent. Both pre-Buddhist schools and the *Yoga Sutras of Patanjali* speak of these heart qualities. Verse thirty-three in the first chapter (*Samadhi Pada*) of the *Yoga Sutras of Patanjali* mentions, 'In relation to happiness, misery, virtue and vice, by cultivating the attitudes of friendliness (*maitri*), compassion (*karuna*), gladness (*mudita*), and indifference (*apekshanam*) respectively, the mind becomes purified and peaceful.'

The Upanishads talk about kindness (*metta*), compassion (*karuna*), and equanimity (*upeksha*). Jain literature mentions all four virtues of the heart. A traditional Tibetan Buddhist prayer summarises the four Immeasurables in the following words:

May all beings have happiness and the cause of happiness.

May they be free of suffering and the cause of suffering.

May they never be disassociated from the supreme happiness, which is without suffering.

May they remain in the boundless equanimity, free from both attachment to close ones and rejection of others.

The four qualities of the heart in Buddhism are called '*Brahmavihara*' in Sanskrit or the 'Abode of Brahma'. *Brahma* refers to the sublime or divine, whereas *vihara* is Sanskrit for monastery or home. Also known as the four Immeasurables or virtues, these qualities are guides for ethical human behaviour and create an atmosphere of compassion, unity, and benevolence. In that these qualities encourage us to delve into whatever conditions we encounter in our lives, they allow us to explore to the very root that which arises with balance and equanimity in friendliness and acceptance. Each quality of the heart is woven into the other, strengthening and nourishing one another as they are cultivated. Often described as basic traits, seen in the eyes and smile and laughter of a baby and the beginner's mind, these virtues get veiled on our journey through life and are forgotten. Below the veil they abide to be awakened.

These qualities of the heart lie at the essence of mindful living. As we cultivate the four foundations of mindfulness on the direct path to liberation, it is our heart that generates how we relate to ourselves and the world that surrounds us. Kindness, compassion, empathetic joy, and equanimity are qualities at the very basis of how we speak, think, and act. They influence our relationships with others, our partner, our family, our friends and loved ones, our colleagues and neighbours, and the human race as a whole.

The mind has a natural tendency to be distracted by the outer world, but the impurities and obstacles must be removed to look within. Emotions like hate, anger, and jealousy trigger the activity of the mind and lead to disturbances in the subconscious that inhibit the mind from becoming single-pointed. We feel jealousy when we see a prosperous person, we rejoice if an enemy suffers, we criticise the virtuous and uphold the deeds of the vicious. In judging and comparing, we move ourselves deeper into a spiral of negative thought patterns. All these impurities of the mind lead us away from our fundamental nature of goodness. No human being wants to suffer. We all want to be happy.

Tibetan Buddhists often describe compassion (love) and wisdom (insight) as the two wings of the awakening heart and mind, sometimes compared to an eagle. It is the embodiment of both, which leads to freedom from the known.

I have experienced the effects of the heart qualities in many retreats and meditations about compassionate living. The heart softens on hearing poetry, a sacred verse, a moving song, or a piece of music, allowing it to become receptive for feelings like friendliness, self-compassion, and connection. It is amazing to witness the effects of a meditation on similarities, especially in settings where competition and difference is part of the success game. It is these experiences of the gentle changes that occur within us, that inspired me to share these insights. Going forward, moving into the hitherto unpredictability of the effects of climate change, temperature swings, storms, and the rising of the oceans, compassion and equanimity will be crucial factors in dealing with the yet unknown consequences we as humanity will have to face.

**

LOVING-KINDNESS

Loving-kindness or unconditional friendliness, also known as 'metta' in Sanskrit/ Pāli, is the first of the virtues expounded upon in the Metta Sutta, the discourse on immeasurable friendliness. Metta emanates from the Sanskrit/ Pāli term *mitra* or *mitta* and is translated as 'friend'. The Metta Sutta, often referred to as the jewel of the teaching, is part of the Sutta Nipata—one of the earliest collections of the Buddha's teachings.

Although metta implies friendliness, care, or concern and is a way of behaviour or state of mind, the essential nature of loving-kindness is a yearning that the person you focus your attention on be well and happy and free from suffering. Loving-kindness carries with it an unconditionality, in that good wishes are bestowed on others without a reason or for fruit of action. The practice of metta directs benevolence, kindness, friendliness, and goodwill to all beings.

The Metta Sutta compares unconditional love to that which parents bestow on their child in the following words:

> Let no one despise anyone anywhere,
> Let no one through anger or hatred
> Wish for others to suffer.
> As a mother would risk her own life
> To protect her child, her only child,

So for all beings one should
Guard one's boundless heart.
(Source: John Peacock, trans. Metta Sutta, from Feldman Christina, Boundless Heart, page 52)

The teachings of the Buddha state that every immeasurable has a so-called direct and indirect opposite or enemy. Near enemies are states that appear similar to the desired quality but actually undermine it. Far enemies are the opposite of what we are trying to achieve. The far enemy of loving-kindness is hatred, often expressed as anger, aversion, or irritation. How do we deal with these emotions? It helps to recognise how painful it is to feel anger or hatred and to understand others' way of seeing. Remembering that all qualities, as well as negative emotions, are transient and all of us possess good, too.

The near enemy is attachment. It shows itself in the conditional love we have for one another, dependent on what we do, say, or feel. In a way it has the air of possessiveness. This is an extremely difficult opponent to tackle as we all suffer from attachment with others. Remind yourself that all is impermanent, you are the object of your attachment and attachment itself. However tough this one is, perhaps it can be addressed by cultivating metta.

The practice of loving-kindness (see Chapter 3) allows us to reap many benefits for the body and the mind. The mind becomes calm and more efficient, leading to a happy mind in a healthy body. Others begin to love, help, and protect you.

The Practice of Metta

This meditation generally consists of silent repetitions of good wishes such as 'may you be happy' or 'may you be free from suffering'.

Although sometimes a bit unnatural to people in the West, the repetition of these simple good wishes goes beyond the verbalisation, in that 'resonance circuits', which connect the emotional and rational areas of the brain are strengthened and activated. We become kinder, more empathetic, and patient with others. The practice of loving-kindness reinforces positivity and helps decrease the negativity so often present in our lives. Its practice leaves us with a deep feeling of joy.

Words or sentences that can be invoked could be the following:

May I/you be happy.
May I/you/ be healthy and free from suffering.
May I/you be safe and secure.
May I/you live in peace and with lightness of Being.

Beginning with oneself, we move to a loved one, then to a neutral person, a person with whom we have had a disagreement and finally widen our awareness to include all sentient beings.

Metta as compassion meditation is practiced the world over by Buddhist monks in the face of calamity, a practice in which collective chanting is carried out, creating a wave of friendliness to resonate in every open heart.

Integrating Loving-Kindness into Daily Life

'Your life is your laboratory,' says Jon Kabat-Zinn. Just as we make mindfulness part of our lives, similarly, we can practice loving-kindness wherever we are. I have silently recited the words of a friendliness meditation before a difficult conversation, a presentation, to the members in a meeting room, to people standing with me in a queue at the supermarket, and to pedestrians on the street. It makes my heart warm and wide in a felt sense of heart connection:

> May you be happy and free from suffering.
> May you be healthy, safe and secure, and live with lightness of being.

COMPASSION

Called *karuna* in Pāli and Sanskrit, compassion results from loving-kindness and seeks to identify other's suffering as one's own. While metta is about the desire for well-being and happiness of others, karuna seeks to remove harm and suffering from others. It is important to distinguish compassion from pity. Pity or sympathetic sorrow seeks to remove suffering, but for a partly selfish (attached) reason; thus, it is not a pure motivation that manifests itself in compassion.

When we look at the near and far enemies of compassion, we find the near enemy is pity and the far enemy is cruelty, hence, totally in opposition to compassion.

Compassion is not possible without kindness and the ability to feel kindness for oneself. Compassion for others require empathy and goodwill and the deep inner willingness to bring suffering and its causes to an end.

The Practice of Compassion

Just as the practice of loving-kindness invokes certain wishes for others, practicing compassion also has specific wishes attached to it, for example:

> May I/you find peace.
> May I/you be safe.
> May I/you find healing.

Integrating Compassion into Daily Life

In the face of the disrupted world we live in, embodying compassion can bring peace to ourselves and our environments. Being able to bring empathy and a change of perspective to feel what the other is going through and doing our best by acting, causes ripples.

When we witness sorrow, it helps to imagine drawing in the grief (sometimes described like a cloud of black smoke) of others, as if breathing it in, and to breath out positive energy (like a body of bright light) and compassion towards the person. This is an adapted practice of the Tibetan Buddhist meditation of Tonglen, also called 'giving and taking'.

EMPATHETIC JOY

Known as '*mudita*' in Sanskrit, empathetic joy is the pleasure arising out of delight in the well-being of others. Sometimes it is compared to the joy of a parent whilst watching their children's success. Empathetic joy has no self-interest attached to it. Empathetic joy meditation is used to cultivate appreciative joy at the success and good fortune of others. Joy at the delight of others, be it an exchange of a smile with a stranger or a bout of laughter in response to others' laughter, is an expression of mudita. It is as if the mirror neurons in our brains are activated and fill us with similar feelings. Mudita is like an inner well of joy that can always be tapped into, under any conditions. Joy surrounds us all the time. Observing others being joyful, partaking in their joy, and recalling the sense of connection—whenever our reservoirs are low—fills the batteries of the heart.

But empathetic joy has enemies, too. The near enemy of joy is exhilaration, the far enemies are jealousy and greed.

In the larger sense of the word, joy is to be found everywhere, especially in the little things that surround us and delight our hearts. Be it a beautiful sunset, inspiring awe, the rays of sunlight falling across my hands as I write this on my laptop, the upright orange tulip in the flower bed, in its intensity of colour or steadfastness, or the joy at an unexpected act of kindness. The unspectacular and subtle trigger, an inner arising of joy in the heart, leading to body sensations of warmth, openness, and tenderness. Our lives are dominated by the cacophony of the loud and unmistakable, which cover-up a recognition of the gentle whispers of little things. Learning to soak up small treasures of pleasure lets joy enter our heart and brain, creating new neuronal pathways that foster a different way of being.

The Practice of Joy

There are many ways to practice empathetic joy or just joy.

We can choose an object that evokes simple, uncomplicated joy, focusing our awareness on anything, no matter how subtle—a sound, a smell, something in nature, an animal, or anything else. What's important is that it allows joy to arise, gently placing our attention on the object for some time, observing it effortlessly. We can let our eyes rest on a flower, a tree in bloom, a butterfly flitting from flower to flower, a work of art, listen to birds chirping or a piece of music, perhaps bathe ourselves in the smell of a flower. We can open our awareness and gaze at a landscape, a range of mountains or rolling hills, the blue sky and the clouds drifting or anything else in nature. Resting with awe and soaking in the quality of joy.

To practise empathetic joy, bring an event to mind that evokes happiness—maybe the birth of a child, a wedding or graduation in the family, a memorable moment with a friend, or a success you recently celebrated. Just allow the feeling of joy and happiness to arise from within. Then repeat the following words to yourself:

> May my happiness continue.
> May my happiness grow.
> May my happiness stay.

Integrating Joy in Our Lives

A beautiful way of allowing the quality of pure joy to enter our way of being, is to be open to pleasant sensations in the body (warmth, tingling, etc.) and in our sensory perception. Remaining aware of subtle, simple, and discreet sounds, aromas, visual impulses, or feelings of contact that generate joy in the body and the heart. Observe expressions of joy in your surroundings—expressions of laughter, of success, of celebrations, or love, and of connectedness and rejoice with others, perhaps bringing a smile of 'co-joy' to your lips.

As the Buddhist teacher Christina Feldman mentions in her book *Boundless Heart*, 'Mindlessness, friendliness, compassion, and joy are like different but interwoven melodies that make up a single song. They are not linear but balance and strengthen one another.'

Joy and gladness are contagious! Smile and the world smiles with you.

EQUANIMITY

This fourth immeasurable is also known as '*upekkha*' in Pāli or '*upeksha*' in Sanskrit. 'Equanimity gives selflessness to metta; gives patience, courage, and fearlessness to compassion; guards joy from sentimentality; and brings all the ennobling qualities of the heart together in liberation,' says Christina Feldman.

Equanimity implies staying calm no matter what life brings to us, be they pleasure and pain, success and failure, or joy and sorrow. Unshakeable like a tree or a mountain, come what may. Equanimity is the gift of poise and balance during chaos and suffering.

The far enemy of equanimity is greed and aversion, the near enemy or that which resembles upekkha but, opposes it, is apathy or indifference. The far enemy of upekkha is greed and resentment, or mind states in obvious opposition. These emotions cause so much distraction in the mind that balance is not possible.

The Practice of Equanimity

How do we make equanimity or balance a part of our lives? In case of deep disturbance when our balance gets shattered by unexpected events or occurrences, becoming aware of what is happening in our bodies, emotions, and thought flow, resting in the flow of the breath, we bring back calmness into our lives. The three-step breathing space described in Chapter 3 is a kind of compact meditation to bring back balance when the waters are rough.

Another alternative is to send out positive wishes to ourselves and others, perhaps with the following words: 'May I learn to experience the arising and passing of all things with equanimity and serenity. May I be open, serene and at peace.'

In recognising that every person is fundamentally like us, wanting happiness and wanting to be free of suffering. In the spirit of equanimity think or whisper to yourself,

'How wonderful would it be if everyone had equanimity, free from attachment, apathy or indifference towards strangers, and hostility or hatred towards those who seem difficult.'

THE STRUCTURE OF MEDITATIONS ON THE FOUR IMMEASURABLES

The meditations for the four Immeasurables follow a distinct system. We begin by directing good wishes to ourselves and then cultivating them for others as well.

Starting by wishing ourselves well, we then proceed by including a friend, then a neutral person, a person with whom we have difficulties, and finally expand our awareness out to include humanity and sentient beings on this planet as a whole.

Why do we begin with ourselves? It is only if we can love and cherish ourselves that we can share this love with others. So, bringing this feeling of connection to our own hearts we till the field for this emotion of unconditional love and friendliness to gently emerge for others. Sometimes it is difficult to bring friendliness to someone with whom we are having a difficult time. It helps to make the difference as small as possible so that the negative aspects do not overwhelm us.

An important aspect lies in awakening a felt sense of friendliness, kindliness, and connection to the person we are wishing well by recalling someone or an emotion that we dearly cherish. Someone who evokes a smile on your face by just thinking of them. Is it possible to feel sensations for feelings like love, respect, compassion, and tenderness in the body? Where are they located and what do they feel like? Allow the warmth, expansiveness, tingling, throbbing feelings to arise . . . are they in your chest, in your heart, in your gut, in your stomach? And then allow these sensations to expand and envelop every cell and pore of your body, your breath, and your entire being. Let this feeling of connection grow outward, beyond the hard edges of your felt body. Sense this positive energy radiating from you outward to all those who you wish well. Remain in silence and stillness with these benevolent feelings and expand them out to reach people who you know, people who you don't know, and all the other sentient beings on this planet. Include the earth in your meditation for a world without divisions and borders, a planet on the cusp of man-made climate destruction.

RESEARCH INTO COMPASSION

Compassion has become an important area of empirical research in the last decade. Empirical research has multiplied in the clinical, medical, translational, and foundational sciences. Studies are investigating numerous aspects of compassion such as the phylogenetic continuity and history of compassion, physiological systems supporting compassion and the impact of compassion on psychological and physical health. Applied studies are looking at the role of compassion in healthcare and educational settings, in organisations, and at training programmes that aim at directing compassion towards oneself and to others in many different contexts.

A tangle within,
A tangle without,
People are entangled in a tangle.
Gotama, I ask you this:
Who can untangle the tangle.
(The Buddha) A person established in virtue,
Developing discernment and mindfulness,
Ardent and clear.
They can untangle this tangle.
Those whose passion, aversion and ignorance
Have faded away.
For them, the tangle is untangled.

—Maurice Walshe, *The Long Discourse of the Buddha:*
A Translation of the Digha Nikaya

Chapter 6
THE SCIENCE BEHIND MINDFULNESS

*N*euroscientific insights into the effectiveness of meditation helped trigger the transition from the religious-spiritual beginnings of mindfulness to the secular context. Mindfulness is now being studied at many universities and research institutions all over the world, and the number of studies has increased exponentially since the early '90s. The Center for Healthy Minds at the University of Wisconsin-Madison, Brown University, which has taken over from the University of Massachusetts Medical Center (home of MBSR programme); the Greater Good Science Center of the University of California, Berkeley; the Oxford Mindfulness Centre; and the Max Planck Institute, Leipzig, are some of the universities at the forefront of scientific research on mindfulness and compassion.

Research on mindfulness has grown enormously in recent decades. Scans have shown that just eight weeks of mindfulness training can change the wiring of the human brain. Neuroplasticity is the technical expression for the continuous reformation of neural pathways in the brain, which can lead to significant behavioural changes, even in old age. At the same time, the grey matter thickens in the regions responsible for learning and memory, emotional regulation, self-referential processing, and perspective thinking.

The brain is made of nearly a hundred billion nerve cells or neurons organised in a network with around a hundred trillion interactions. As we encounter something for the first time, the dendrites—thread-like projections of the neurons—make connections with dendrites of other neurons, and a neural pathway is created. For instance, when people start playing an instrument or learning a new skill, new connections are formed in their brains. And if they practise the piano several times, the connections become stronger and stronger. In addition to new connections being formed, the brain starts to grow entirely new neurons to accommodate the newly acquired skill. As we continue to practise, the neurons need to push further apart to accommodate these new connections, and the brain expands.

In a study published in *Scientific American*, neuroscientist Eleonore Maguire from the University College, London, researched into whether London taxi drivers also had larger-than-average hippocampi. To earn their license, taxi drivers in training spend three to four years driving around the city on mopeds, memorising a labyrinth of 25,000 streets within a 10-kilometer radius of Charing Cross train station, as well as thousands of tourist attractions and hot spots. 'The Knowledge', as it is called, is unique to London taxi licensing and involves a series of gruelling exams that only about 50 per cent of hopefuls pass.

The study that monitored taxi drivers for a period of four years in London, showed that the part of the brain that navigates spatial intelligence—the hippocampus—enlarges over time. The brain is just like a muscle and mental exercise of any kind is akin to a workout, creating changes in the brain's structure. The study confirmed that cognitive exercise produces physical changes in the brain.

It also showed you can produce profound changes in the brain with training.

Extensive research has been performed using neuroimaging and musical training, providing evidence in favour of training-related plasticity. Cross-sectional studies identified structural and functional differences between the brains of musicians and non-musicians in regions related to motor control and auditory processing, the primary motor and premotor areas, parietal areas, and the fibre tracts connecting them.

A well-known study at Harvard Medical School got a group of people to practise the piano for an hour a day for five days, at the end of which they were asked to go through an MRI brain scanner. As expected, areas of the brain associated with fine motor movement and differentiating sounds were thicker after the practise, with more neurons and connections compared to the period before piano practise. There was a second group of people who spent an hour a day for five days imagining themselves playing the piano, without ever actually touching a keyboard. And at the end of the five days, when this second group got their brains scanned, what do you think the researchers found? The same areas of the brain that had grown in the first group had increased in the second group! There was no difference between the groups. This demonstrated that both the mental rehearsal as well as actual physical practise create neuroplastic changes in the brain. Isn't it fascinating?

This is significant because we practise 'default mode' most of the time. The default mode network (DMN) is a network of interacting brain regions that is active when a person is not focused on the outside world, which is measurable with the functional magnetic resonance imaging (fMRI) technique. The network includes several high-level cognitive areas such as the medial prefrontal cortex (mPFC), posterior cingulate cortex (PCC), and parietal regions (PTL) of the brain. DMN is mostly known as the 'task negative' network where regions show strongly correlated activity at rest and are deactivated during cognitive goal-directed tasks.

As outlined earlier, when we are not paying attention to something, we switch off into mind-wandering and automatic pilot. This then gets hardwired into the brain, and we become even more likely to remain in this mode. When we practice mindfulness, different parts of the brain are activated. These areas then become stronger and thicker, and we start experiencing these patterns of activation spontaneously. People who practice mindfulness meditation find that they naturally start catching themselves in the default mode throughout the day. And any time we catch ourselves in the default mode, we are no longer on autopilot. Simultaneously, because of the use-it-or-lose-it nature of neuroplasticity, the parts of the brain associated with default mode become weaker and eventually start to disappear. In this way, practicing mindfulness literally changes our brain.

NEUROSCIENTIFIC FINDINGS

The development of imaging techniques, such as MRI, has been providing high-resolution images of the brain structure since the mid-1980s and making visible and verifiable what happens in the brain through mindfulness meditation. Scientific research focuses—among other things—on the positive effects of mindfulness on health and well-being, on emotion regulation, on relationship, on experience, and on cognitive abilities, which are important in the work process. The short- and long-term effects of meditation have also been investigated on the level of psychic states and personality traits.

Neuroscientific studies have mainly been able to identify areas of the brain whose activity correlate with observed effects that occur with regular meditation practice. What correlations have been established so far?

- The almond nucleus (amygdala) shrinks, resulting in reduced activity, leading to a reduced anxiety response
- The brain substance grows leading to more attention performance. Furthermore, there is an activation of the anterior cingulate cortex (ACC)
- The hippocampus grows, which is related to the improvement of memory performance
- Activation and structural change of the insula correlates with the improvement of awareness and empathy
- Overactivity of the default mode network (DMN) results in increased worrying, rumination, and depression. Meditation shows lower activity leading to an improvement in the above symptoms
- Reduced amygdala activity, prefrontal cortex activation, and improved connectivity lead to improved emotional regulation.

THE AMYGDALA AND ITS ROLE IN THE BODY

You may wonder what the amygdala is and where it is situated in the brain. The Amygdala is a collection of nuclei found deep within the temporal lobe. The term amygdala comes from Latin and translates to 'almond' as it has an almond-like shape. There are two amygdalae, one in each cerebral hemisphere.

The amygdala is part of brain structures referred to collectively as the limbic system, which are known to play important roles in emotion and behaviour. It is best known for its role in the processing of fear and triggers the fight, freeze, or flight reaction.

When we are confronted with a frightening stimulus, information about it is quickly conveyed to the amygdala, which can then send signals to parts of the brain such as the hypothalamus, triggering a fight-or-flight reaction (e.g., increased heart rate and respiration to prepare for action, hormonal release, tensing of muscles, etc.).

According to research studies, information regarding potentially terrifying objects in the environment can reach the amygdala before we are even aware that there is anything to be afraid of. The thalamus connects to the amygdala, and sensory information concerning arousing stimuli may be conveyed via this pathway to the amygdala before being processed consciously by the cerebral cortex. This enables the initiation of a fear response before we have a chance to even consider what is so frightening.

If you are truly in danger, this type of reflex can be beneficial. If you're strolling through the grass and a snake pops out unexpectedly, you don't want to have to spend a lot of time thinking about how dangerous the snake is. Instead, you want your body to feel immediate dread and react by jumping away and standing still without having to think about it.

The amygdala appears to be crucial in the formation of memories linked with fear-inducing situations, in addition to its role in the onset of a fear response. It is known from experiments conducted with mice, that if you take mice with an intact amygdala and play a tone right before you give them a foot shock, they will quickly begin to associate the tone with the unpleasant shock. The mice begin to show a fear reaction (e.g., freezing in place) as soon as the tone is played—but before the shock is initiated. Mice with lesions to the amygdala showed a reduced ability to remember that the sound came before the shock. These mice will continue their business and the sound has no negative associations for them.

A practice of mindfulness causes a restructuring of the neural pathways in the brain. This leads to a change in mental patterns by creating new neural pathways. The formation of new paths leads to new behaviours and attitudes that in turn lead to different perspectives and a departure from our deeply ingrained mental habits.

'We can use our mind to change our brain to change our minds' is a phrase coined by neurophysiologist Dr Rick Hanson. Regular brain training does this for our mental abilities, which is the equivalent of fitness for physical health. 'Neurons that fire together, wire together.' This is also known as Hebb's Rule on synaptic plasticity, which was postulated by the Canadian cognitive Psychobiologist Donald O. Hebb.

Moreover, the hormones released during a stress reaction triggered by the amygdala—a state we were nearly constantly in during the beginning of the pandemic—result in a cocktail in our system that rarely gets a chance to dissolve. Each new stressor promotes the release of stress hormones adrenalin and cortisol along with all the associated bodily reactions. Hormones that strengthen the nurturing part of our brain like oxytocin or endorphins take a back seat, and the connection with ourselves and others becomes more difficult.

An inbuilt 'negativity bias', which has resulted out of our 'being on the edge' through evolution is a result of being hunters and gatherers in surroundings full of danger for our lives. Our brains tend to focus, by default, on negative information and dwells on threats. This bias towards negative thinking explains why we thrive on sensationalist news and media. Neuroscientists estimate that it takes a tenth of a second to notice a threat, for example, a shadow in the dark or a disturbing noise, and much longer to become aware of something that pleases us. Everything threatening goes straight into the memory where it can be immediately recalled if needed. It is estimated that it takes five pleasant experiences to balance a single negative occurrence of the same dimension. So, to counterbalance something negative, we need to appreciate so many more awe-inspiring occurrences.

Neuropsychologist Dr Rick Hanson describes the brain being like a 'Velcro' or sticky for all that is negative and 'Teflon' or slippery for all that is positive. Our hormone system also reflects this bias. The hormones adrenalin, cortisol, and norepinephrine—which are released when the body encounters stress or negative experiences—have powerful effects on the body so that we can react instantaneously. Hormones like oxytocin—the 'cuddle hormone'—or endorphins—the body's own painkiller—are much softer and gentler even though they foster well-being, healing, and our sense of connection.

When we balance the negative and the positive by dwelling on the pleasant, we allow our brains to rewire and create neurons that are responsible for evoking feelings of happiness and joy. The neuroplasticity of the brain allows us to change it for the better and for us to flourish.

Psychologist Paul Gilbert, known for his work on *The Compassionate Mind*, describes the process of 'Neurogenesis'. Our brains produce new brain cells or neurons every day, demonstrating how active the brain is. It was believed, although for a long time, that neurogenesis only occurred at the embryonic stage. But now we know that it continues through adulthood and gently declines with age. So, always remember to turn towards the positive, bringing in beauty and awe at the unspectacular but omnipresent into your life. Just focusing on something beautiful, be it a sunset, a piece of music, a work of art or a flower for fifteen seconds allows areas for positivity to be generated in the brain and our attitude to switch to appreciation.

It is in times of crisis that we require the stabilising power of meditation and mindfulness more than ever before to let us steer the wheel of life with calm when in troubled waters.

Once we realise the opportunity of meditation and practicing mindfulness, the potential for learning and changing ingrained behaviours becomes limitless.

The breeze at dawn has secrets to tell you.
Don't go back to sleep.
You must ask for what you really want.
Don't go back to sleep.
People are going back and forth across the doorsill
Where the two worlds touch.
The door is round and open.
Don't go back to sleep.

—*Rumi (transl. by Coleman Barks in
The Essential Rumi)*

Chapter 7
BENEFITS OF MINDFULNESS
AND MEDITATION

You may wonder why I am including a section on the benefits of meditation in this handbook. In today's science-dominated society every practice needs to be proven by evidence-based data in order to find acceptance in the intellectual, fact-driven mind. Positive effects include the impact on health, stress, cognitive functioning, emotional and social intelligence, and ageing.

The research on the impact of meditation has increased manifold since the first studies were conducted. These consisted of observing different meditation techniques. In the '70s, systematic research was first conducted on the effects of transcendental meditation. The American Mindfulness Research Association (AMRA) annually compiles the number of publications in the field of mindfulness. In the year 2000 AMRA recorded ten studies, and in 2020 close to 1,200 studies have been published. Most research focus on the effects of the eight-week MBSR programme and other mindfulness-based interventions (MBI) in healthcare. As the application of mindfulness in many fields spreads, an increasing number of research studies are being carried out on the application of mindfulness in organisations, education, relationships, emotional intelligence, and brain and immune system to name a few.

A concise review of current scientific evidence shows that both higher levels of trait mindfulness as well as mindfulness training led to better psychological well-being, coping, and quality of life. MBIs have been found to produce significant effects in alleviating the burden of stress-related diseases like coronary artery disease, fibromyalgia, cancer, irritable bowel syndrome, chronic pain, psoriasis, depression, and many more.

The interest of HH the Dalai Lama in bringing the evidence of modern science to the ancient techniques of Eastern philosophy further encouraged research into this area. The establishment of institutions like the Mind & Life Institute and the position of influential meditation teachers and scientists like Jon Kabat-Zinn, Richard Davidson, Daniel Goleman, Joseph Goldstein, and many others have supported this quest—also in the interest of their own work.

In *Altered Traits* by neuroscientist Richard Davidson from the University of Wisconsin and psychologist and emotional intelligence expert Daniel Goleman examined all publications on mindfulness. They found that only 1 per cent of papers withstood the rigorous standards of clinical trials. These studies showed that four attributes clearly improve with meditation, which are: Focus, memory performance, serenity in stressful situations, and the interpersonal component of coexistence.

I have summarised the numerous publications and have tried to focus on the main effects hitherto proven by evidence-based studies.

MEDITATION AND ITS EFFECTS

Mindfulness-based practices have several effects on mind and body:

a) Meditation lowers both the heart rate and blood pressure, thus reducing the risk of cardiovascular diseases.
b) Meditation lowers one's breathing rate and reduces muscle tension.
c) It lowers the risk of inflammatory diseases as meditation reduces the concentration of certain proteins in the blood that play a role in such diseases. The concentrations of the hormone cortisone have been found to reduce.
d) Chronic pain can be helped by a drop in pain sensitivity. Programmes that specifically address the mental and emotional response to pain (like MBSR) or use the breath to gently soothe the pain (mindfulness-based pain management) complement other pain-reducing strategies.
e) Meditation increases stress resistance, hence, reducing the effects of worry, anxiety, and burnout on the body.
f) Mindfulness strengthens the immune system. A seminal study found that, after just eight weeks of training, mindfulness meditation increases our system's ability to fight off illnesses.
g) Mindfulness exercises support the deep-sleep phase and help calm the mind. Practicing mindfulness and meditation may improve our sleep quality.
h) Mindfulness and meditation practitioners have a stronger sense of self and seem to act more in line with their values. They may also have a healthier body image, more secure self-esteem, and more resilience to negative feedback.

i) MBCT was designed by psychotherapy researchers and cognitive-behavioural therapists Zindel V. Segal, J. Mark G. Williams, and John D. Teasdale to prevent relapse in depression. This structured eight-week course is widely prescribed by the National Institute for Health and Clinical Excellence in the UK. A recent study has shown that MBSR is as effective as a commonly used first-line antidepressant in the treatment of adults with anxiety disorders.

j) A lot of research has gone into the application of mindfulness for the reduction of addictive behaviours, especially for smoking cessation, alcoholism, gaming, and gambling. The use of app-based MBI programmes are cost-effective, easily accessible, and increase compliance. In smokers, they have been shown to be effective in reducing craving-induced smoking. The combination of MBIs with other treatment approaches is showing promise.

k) The aging process of cells are known to be reduced, as the health and resilience of the chromosomes are improved by mindfulness techniques. This science called Epigenetics is at the forefront of science today.

MEDITATION AND COGNITIVE FUNCTION

Mindfulness is good for our minds. Several studies have found that mindfulness increases positive emotions while reducing stress and negative emotions. Mental symptoms such as anxiety, as the anxiety are less active. Mindfulness exercises are also used to treat anxiety disorders.

Mindfulness changes the structure of our brains. Research has found that it increases the density of grey matter in brain regions linked to learning, memory, emotion regulation, and empathy.

Mindfulness helps us focus. Studies suggest that mindfulness helps one tune out distractions and improves our memory, attention skills, and decision-making abilities.

MEDITATION AND EMOTIONAL INTELLIGENCE

Mindfulness fosters compassion and altruism. Research suggests that mindfulness training makes us more likely to help someone in need and increases activity in neural networks involved in understanding the suffering of others and regulating emotions. Evidence suggests it might boost self-compassion as well.

We know today that the future workplace will require employees with high emotional intelligence skills at all levels of the organisation. With the rise of automation, machine learning, and artificial intelligence, the line between tasks a machine can do and a human being is capable of will blur. Our uniqueness as human beings—whose cognitive, emotional, and social skills are irreplaceable—will be a must-have at the workplace going forward. Mindfulness enhances these skills and competencies.

MEDITATION AND ORGANISATIONS

Mindfulness training is good for work as it could help make leaders more confident, improve creativity, reduce multitasking, and improve client satisfaction. Especially in organisations, people need to be able to process complex information quickly and efficiently. The ability of 'out-of-the-box' thinking in solving a problem, with the application of new and creative mental categories, is improved by mindfulness. Psychologist Ellen Langer was able to confirm that mindfulness facilitates the development of new cognitive structures. Langer found that after a mindfulness training session, her investigators were able to look at standard tasks with a fresh look. This ability of the 'beginner spirit' is a central principle of mindfulness (see Chapter 4).

Distraction and a wandering mind are reduced by mindfulness practices as well. Studies have shown that up to 47 per cent of the time our mind is not where it should be. People who can concentrate better show increased performance. The risk of low focus was described by one executive as, 'When my mind drifts in a meeting, I wonder what business opportunity I just missed.'

People who practice mindfulness have a better working memory, which is the short-term memory that processes current thought processes. In a working environment, better memory performance can strengthen complex ideas for strategic work, problem-solving, or even intensive collaboration. A less active amygdala also leads to more rest and less irritability and that means clarity.

MINDFULNESS AND PARENTING

Mindfulness has been proven to be good for parents and parents-to-be. Studies suggest that mindfulness may reduce pregnancy-related anxiety, stress, and depression in expectant parents, and may even reduce the risk of premature births and developmental issues. Parents who practice mindful parenting report less stress, more positive parenting practices, and better relationships with their children, and the children, in turn, are less susceptible to depression and anxiety and have better social skills. Mindfulness training for families may lead to less-stressed parents who pay more attention to their children.

MINDFULNESS EFFECTS TRAITS

Altered Traits by scientists Richard Davidson and Daniel Goleman looked into traits that long-term meditation has proven to change. The authors concluded that even just two weeks of practice improves attention, leading to better focus, less mind-wandering, and improved working memory. It was also found that markers for inflammation lessen slightly after just thirty hours of practice. For those who have meditated for over 1,000 hours, there are brain and hormonal indicators of lowered reactivity to stress. Compassion meditation brings an attunement with people who are suffering and a greater likelihood of help. The length of meditation practice plays a distinct role in the development of changed traits in different cognitive skills, social and emotional behaviour, and specific health parameters.

Many of the effects described above have resulted in the application of mindfulness and meditation in numerous settings, from psychology and medicine to education, politics, and the workplace.

A Zen Story

A wise old Zen master was once asked by his followers, 'Sire, what is your secret to be happy and content? We would like to be as happy as you are.'

The old man replied with a smile, 'When I lie down, I lie down. When I get up, I get up. When I walk, I walk, and when I eat, I eat.'

The followers were somewhat puzzled. Then one excalimed, 'Please do not tease us. We have been practicing exactly what you just mentioned. We sleep, we eat, and we walk. But we are not happy. So, tell us your secret!'

The master gave the same answer: 'When I lie down, I lie down. When I get up, I get up. When I walk, I walk, and when I eat, I eat.'

Feeling the restlessness and displeasure of his seekers, the master added after a while, 'I am sure you also lie down, and you walk, and you eat. But whilst you are lying down, you are also thinking about getting up. Whilst getting up, you think about where you are going, and whilst you are walking, you ask yourself what you are going to eat. Your thoughts are always somewhere else and not there... where you are. In the intersection between the past and the future is where life takes place. Surrender to this unmeasurable moment fully and you will have the chance to be genuinely happy and content.'

The secret of health for both mind and body is not to mourn for the past, worry about the future, or anticipate troubles, but to live in the present moment wisely and earnestly.
—**The Buddha**

Part II
All about Meditation

Chapter 8
THE ART OF MEDITATION

The mystery and art of meditation has been described and practiced since time immemorial by different traditions, religions, and cultures in a multitude of forms. Be it in the form of prayer, contemplation, devotional song, music, dance, poetry, art, paced walking, or just sitting in silence, people have connected to the universal essence of existence in houses of prayer or individually for centuries.

Meditation is a lifelong encounter with oneself, uncovering layers of understanding of the outer nature of ourselves in a process of self-discovery. Meditation continues after the formal practise session is over, in our daily life, our relationships, life's ups and downs, and in emotionally and physically difficult situations. That is where real meditation begins.

Meditation cultivates our capacity to be more awake, present, curious, and responsive. Our qualities for compassion, loving-kindness, joy, equanimity, and resilience are developed and trained, leading to attitudinal changes in our relationships towards ourselves and towards others.

By connecting to the underlying awareness, we meditate; by strengthening our focus, we meditate; by opening the vast space of open awareness, we meditate until the relationship with the innermost part of our being becomes a constant companion.

As the great Persian poet, jurist, Islamic scholar, and theologian Rumi said: 'I have lived on the lip of insanity, wanting to know reasons, knocking on a door. It opens. I've been knocking from the inside.'

Meditation is the key to the eternal within, that which remains when the body drops, that which is not born and does not die. It is only in the stillness within, that insights can arise through the wisdom of the heart, which reveals the mystery of existence. The mind and intellect are instruments of reason that we cater to in schools, universities, and other places of intellectual understanding. True intuition can only arise from the essence of being. Once discovered, digested, and imbibed they become heart wisdom, often leading to a profound sense of silence. This is the other form of intelligence, which springs from the fountainhead within you, suggests Rumi.

Meditation can also be used to train the mind. Just as we train the body, the mind can be trained beyond just gathering and storing information. A workout of the mind enhances clarity, focus, and decision-making. Perhaps you have observed the activity of your mind in a moment of silence. Been astounded by the transient flow of thoughts, the rise of emotions and feelings, images and judgements which go hand in hand. Often scattered, totally inconsistent ideas and beliefs, fantasies and speculations, worries and fears are watched. Haphazard movements in the mind, arising, here for a while, then dissolving to leave no trace. You can compare the mind to a snow globe, shake it and the snowflakes disperse and float around, disturbing the liquid. Once you put the snow globe down, the flakes slowly settle to the base and the liquid becomes still and clear.

All great traditions have practised meditation in some form or the other. A new wave of classical studies is exploring the role of ancient Greek philosophy as a form of psychotherapeutic intervention. The Stoic practice of attention or 'concentration in the present moment' is akin to meditation and mindfulness. Stoicism owes its name to the 'painted porch' (Stoa Poikile, ancient Greek), a colonnade overlooking the central square of Athens, where merchant-turned philosopher Zeno of Citium (334 – 262 BC) gathered with his disciples to discuss his ideas. Zeno had been influenced by the teachings of Socrates, which is why Stoicism is remembered as a major Socratic school. Stoicism became the foremost school of philosophy among the educated elite in the Hellenistic world and the Roman Empire.

The Christian church has always had a rich underlying meditative tradition within the order of monks and nuns. By the 4th century, groups of Christians, who came to be called the Desert Fathers (early Christian hermits and ascetics, who lived in the Scetes desert of the Roman province of Egypt), had sought God in the deserts of Palestine and Egypt, and led to an early model of monastic Christian life. The tradition of a Christian life of 'constant prayer' in a monastic setting was first seen here.

Beginning in the Middle Ages, Christian meditation moved from vocal prayer in both the Western and Eastern Christian monastic traditions. Two separate and different meditation techniques emerged as a result: The formal method of scriptural prayer called 'Lectio Divina' in the Western Church and 'Hesychasm' in the Eastern Church. Hesychasm involved the repetition of the Jesus Prayer, 'Lord Jesus Christ, son of God, have mercy on me, a sinner.' Lectio Divina, consisted of reading, meditating, praying, and contemplating different scripture passages.

Daily life in a Benedictine monastery consisted of prayer, work, and the reading of the Bible or Lectio Divina in the spirit of Ora et labora (i.e., pray and work). This form of a slow and thoughtful reading of the scripture and the ensuing pondering of its meaning was a form of meditation. Bernard of Clairvaux played a crucial role in reiterating the significance of Lectio Divina within the Cistercian order at the start of the 12th century.

A great figure from the 13th Century, Albertus Magnus, believed that the aim of life was union with God and that contemplation was the path to attain it. He wrote: 'When thou prayest, shut thy door; this is, the door of the senses. Keep them barred and bolted against all phantasms, and images. Nothing pleases God more than a mind free from all occupations and distractions . . . He who penetrates into himself and so transcends himself, ascends truly to God.'

Western Christian meditation was further developed by saints such as Ignatius of Loyola and Teresa of Avila in the 16th century. Many great saints like Hildegard of Bingen, St Francis of Assisi, St John of the Cross, Meister Eckhart, Pierre Teilhard de Chardin, and more have written about their experiences of meditation and the inner vision of Christ.

The early 20th century witnessed a revival in the practice of meditation with the use of the Lectio Divina being emphasised in one of the principal documents of the Second Vatican Council, the dogmatic constitution *Dei verbum* (Latin for 'Word of God').

Pope Francis, in an address to the general audience in 2021, mentioned meditation as a need for everyone. He stated that 'the ancients used to say that the organ of prayer is the heart.'

Christians base their spiritual life on prayer. True prayer—which is direct communion with God—is a meditative state. Prayer has distinct phases. Vocal prayer is accompanied by listening and liturgical prayer. This is followed by discursive prayer (meditation or reflection on the text), affective prayer, and the prayer of simplicity. This first phase is active prayer. There follows the prayer of stillness. The second phase termed passive prayer involves contemplation and culminates in the prayer of unity, also known as the prayer of the heart or 'Jesus prayer'.

Prayer beads or the Rosary are used for meditation in the Christian faith. The gentle repetition of the prayers allows a shift into deeper states of meditation. Rosaries are used by members of the Catholic Church, the Eastern Orthodox Church, the Lutherans, and as Anglican prayer beads of the Episcopalian tradition for prayer and meditation.

There are several references to meditation in the Old and New Testaments of the Bible:

Be still and know that I am God.
—*Psalms 46:10*
The kingdom of God lies within you.
—*Luke 17:21*

These are the direct references to meditation, calling on man to still his mind and dive deep into himself to discover the peace and tranquillity of the kingdom of God.

Sufi meditation is a central component of Islamic spirituality. The Sufi tradition centres on developing a personal relationship with God through self-knowledge and self-inquiry. It uses *Zikr* (chanting or remembrance) and *Muraqabah* (meditation or transcendental union with God) to empty the mind and heart. The journey of the Sufi is the journey of a lover returning to the arms of the beloved. In order to be one with him, the ego has to die. The way of the Sufi is the way of the heart.

Sufism is known to have originated before the 6th Century AD, when Prophet Mohammed was living and preaching. It is accepted that the Sufis had their origins in the science of the Magi, an ancient group of magicians and seers who lived in Persia around 4000 BC. The Aryan invaders elevated the Magi to the priesthood of the new pantheistic Aryan religion because of their wisdom and knowledge.

The Sufis are well-known for their wandering dervishes or renunciates of the Islamic world. The dervishes wander as part of their practice, working to fully know the mind in their quest for God realisation. They are known for their ecstatic trance states attained through dancing and chanting. In India the famous bard Kabir was a Sufi. The wandering minstrels of Bengal, the Bauls, sing and chant the most beautiful poetry in the name of Allah to the point of attaining cosmic ecstasy. The Sufi mystic, poet, and philosopher Rumi of the 13th Century is one of the most famous wisdom writers of all times, as is his teacher Hafeez.

Sufism can be described as an attitude or state of physical, mental, and spiritual harmony and union with the cosmos, which adapts itself and continuously evolves to suit the necessities of the time and place.

Meditation among the Sufis spans dance and moving meditations and sitting meditations techniques that use powerful mantras and sounds. The most important aspect of Sufi meditation is the ability to open up, to remove all inhibitions and restraints from a personality to enable a surrender to the fullness of life. The embodiment in practical living is the basis on which the 'clearing of the soul' is facilitated by meditative exercises—sometimes in combination with dance or music and sometimes using introspection. Sufis are often seen whirling, and as they move, they recite a continuous mantra, which permeates their entire being. Sufis also use the power of breath in meditation.

Storytelling is an aspect of Sufism that allows the attitude to life take shape in the consciousness of the seeker. These stories can be interpreted at many levels of understanding and often the comprehension of a story indicates the level of developmental awareness of the listener. One person may find a story intriguing, another will grasp different layers of the story and laugh out loud, a third may smile knowingly, comprehending the full dimensions and truth embodied in the story.

In most Sufi stories, the main character is the legendary Mullah Nasreddin, who usually plays the role of the fool. The fool is the wise man at play. Sufi stories often have seven distinct layers of meaning, and these are simultaneously clear to the enlightened listener.

The following story, as an example, is a path to awaken us to the blind spots inherent in the normal patterns of perception in daily life:

> One-night Nasreddin and his wife woke to hear two men fighting outside their window. She sent Mullah to find out what the trouble was. He wrapped his blanket around his shoulders and went outside. As soon as he approached the men, one of them snatched his blanket and they both ran off.
> 'What was the fighting about?' his wife asked as the Mullah entered the bedroom.
> 'I think they must have been fighting about my blanket because when they got it, they stopped fighting and ran away,' replied Nasreddin.

In Hinduism, meditation or *dhyana* is first mentioned in the ancient Vedic texts. Recent archaeological excavations in the Indus Valley, in the Harappan-Mohenjo-daro culture, dating to 3500 BCE have found steatite seals depicting figures seated in a meditation-like posture, which predates the Vedas by centuries. Several Upanishads expound upon meditation. In Chandogya Upanishad, one of the oldest Upanishads, there is a powerful description of meditation:

> 'Meditation (Dhyana) indeed is greater than the mind. The earth, as it were, meditates. The atmosphere, as it were, meditates. Heaven, as it were, meditates. The waters, as it were, meditate. The mountains, as it were, meditate. Both men and gods, as it were, meditate. He who worships God (Brahman) as meditation, as far as meditation extends, so far does he gain the power to act as he wills.'
> —Chandogya Upanishad VII.7

Do we not hear the same message that mindfulness reveals? Meditation is an important aspect of the philosophy of Advaita Vedanta, which holds that God exists already within man's own nature, and it is the realisation thereof that brings liberation. The path of liberation can be achieved only through spiritual knowledge and the knowledge obtained through direct insight and inquiry into one's own nature of pure consciousness. Vedantic philosophy uses the process of gyana yoga or the path of inquiry.

Dvaita is a theistic school of thought, which propounds that God exists external to man's present condition but can be attained by constant loyalty and devotion to his form and name. This path is called bhakti yoga, or the path of devotion.

The teachings of Vedanta have a three-pronged trail:

1. Deep inner listening and hearing with an open and receptive heart and mind (*shravana*),
2. Deep contemplation and thinking about what has been heard (*manana*) with the intent to understand oneself, and
3. Consistent meditation thereupon (*nididhyasana*) until full realisation dawns, which is a state of samadhi or transcendent awareness.

The repeated practise of self-examination and self-remembrance is an essential aspect of Vedantic meditation. Vedanta recommends different methods of meditation depending on one's temperament, the nature and life circumstances, especially for lay meditators focusing on individual practice and relative to the level of each practitioner.

Vedantic meditation is highly diverse and generally private, emphasising individual practice over group practice, having no specific formulas. At the core of Vedanta lies the practice of individual self-enquiry, as expounded by the great sages like Ramana Maharshi, Nisargadatta Maharaj, Aurobindo, Swami Rama, and Ramakrishna.

In the Vedantic philosophy of knowledge and meditation, all limbs of yogic philosophy merge, be they the paths of service (karma yoga), devotion (bhakti yoga), posture and breath (hatha yoga and pranayama), or knowledge (jnana yoga). All paths are required to reach self-realisation.

Many meditations begin with a focus on an external object or the breath to quietly focus the mind. Initially when you sit in silence you will notice that your thought flow increases rapidly. With time the mind will still and slowly you will begin to observe your thoughts and emotions, without being dragged into them. Like ripples on the surface of the ocean.

One example of Vedantic meditation is *Trataka*, which involves focusing on a single point or flame of a candle or on a deity like Shiva, Krishna, or Buddha. It is also possible to meditate on an object like the sky or on the sun. The essential meditative process—the maintenance of a single focus—is the same whatever be the object. This form of meditation is subjective, also called '*upasana*' (worship). Here, willpower is used to focus the consciousness on the object. In Buddhism this method is called Shamatha. Another form of meditation is '*nididhyasana*' (seeking the source) in which the source of consciousness is explored, termed as Vipassana in Buddhism.

The great Indian master Patanjali, in his most well-known work, put together the theory, science, and practice of yoga and meditation in the Yoga Sutras. Written between the 2nd and 4th Century BC, the Yoga Sutras consist of 196 sutras or aphoristic statements that describe yoga philosophy and the mind, also known as ashtanga yoga or raja yoga. The eight limbs are defined as *yama* (abstinence), *niyama* (observance), *asana* (pose), *pranayama* (the practice of controlling the vital force, usually through control of the breath), *dharana* (concentration), *dhyana* (meditation) and *samadhi* (self-realisation, absorption) according to *The Yoga Sutras of Patanjali* by Satchidananda Swami.

Patanjali defines meditation as that state 'when the mind becomes free from the awareness of subjective and objective experience'. Only then meditation dawns.

When external images, sounds, and senses no longer distract you, you are in a state of meditation. The meditator remains acutely awake and aware, but the awareness is taken away from the external world. The mind is controlled and effortlessly focused on one point, having transcended normal limitations of the mind and in complete oneness with the object of concentration.

The Yoga Sutras of Patanjali are categorised into four main parts, each with an intention behind the selected sutras:

1. *Samadhi pada* (defining what yoga is and enlightenment)
2. *Sadhana pada* (the connection between student and the higher Self)
3. *Vibhuti pada* (dedication to the practice and self-discipline)
4. *Kaivalya pada* (liberation or freedom from suffering)

From these primary categories, the yoga student is guided through the obstacles that may occur on the path towards enlightenment and different solutions to deal with them. The goal of Patanjali's Yoga Sutras is to reconnect the seeker's mind and soul back to the subtler aspects of the physical body through self-reflection, mantras, and spiritual practices.

Although only a small fraction practice meditation today, it was once an important part of every Hindu's way of life. Children were initiated into yoga and meditation at an early age (as I was) and they were taught breathing exercises and mantras. These practices were aimed at developing different centres of the brain and to harmonise the growth of the physical, mental, and emotional parts of a child's body. Yoga was practiced throughout one's life.

In schools of Buddhism, the terms 'shamatha' and 'vipassana' denote these two aspects of meditation. Shamatha often translated as 'tranquillity of the mind' or 'peaceful abiding' is an introductory practice that seeks to stabilise the mind by cultivating a steady awareness of the object of meditation. Most often, the breath is used as the focus of a practice.

Shamatha meditation allows us to experience our mind as it is. We see that our minds are full of thoughts once we sit in silence. Some thoughts are agreeable, others not so much to our liking, and some are neutral. Living as we do, in a world packed with distraction and experiencing, it is normal to run into a busy and active mind. Practicing shamatha meditation over time calms our thoughts and feelings. We encounter peace of mind and abide by our feelings as they are. Eventually, this leads to a decrease in difficult thoughts and emotions as these are dissolved by the breath, like bubbles arising on the surface of a pot that burst on contact with air.

Once we experience stable awareness, we are then ready to develop insight into the basis of mind and self with the practice of vipassana, by investigating the intrinsic nature of thoughts themselves, like heat is the nature of fire.

Vipassana or insight meditation is the practice of continued close attention to sensation, which ultimately leads to the true nature of existence. Focusing on the rising and falling of the abdomen, as an example, sensations will arise in the world of the senses, emotions, thoughts and so on. In vipassana meditation these are taken note of, labelled, and allowed to recede. Labelling helps us to perceive the actual nature of our experience. In the course of time, from within us, aspects about our true nature are revealed.

Religions, or spiritual disciplines, have each propounded their own techniques of meditation. They are like different gates that open to the same road with many parallel lanes with the same goal. These techniques teach you how to begin meditation, by opening different doors to meditative awareness. Regular meditation practice is required to maintain this way of being in contact with ourselves.

On this profound path, you will witness yourself developing and expanding and you will be able to see your potentialities blossoming as your inner life unfolds. Daily life will begin to inspire you and you will live every moment to the fullest. Your inner and outer life will complement and enrich another.

Meditation is important for anyone who wants to become more alert in the mind and the body. It can be practiced by all, at every stage and moment. As meditation leads to a healthy body and a steady focused mind, the practice is of great benefit. A mind that does not waver, one that remains grounded in the face of changing circumstances, environments, and growing uncertainty is a steady mind that is required now more than ever before.

The following chapters will give you an overview of different requirements for meditation like choosing a meditation space, body posture, preparing for a longer practice with breathing exercises, mindful movement or simple chair yoga, common obstacles that can hinder your practice, and how you can deal with them.

Some of the meditations in this collection are based on practices from MBSR and contemporary secular meditations, which I use regularly in my meditation classes.

Moko Kahan Dhundhere Bande
Mein To Tere Paas Mein
Na Teerath Mein, Na Moorat Mein
Na Ekant Niwas Mein
Na Mandir Mein, Na Masjid Mein
Na Kabe Kailas Mein
Mein To Tere Paas Mein Bande
Mein To Tere Paas Mein
Na Mein Jap Mein, Na Mein Tap Mein
Na Mein Barat Upaas Mein
Na Mein Kiriya Karm Mein Rehta
Nahin Jog Sanyas Mein
Nahin Pran Mein Nahin Pind Mein
Na Brahmand Akas Mein
Na Mein Prakuti Prawar Gufa Mein
Nahin Swasan Ki Swans Mein
Khoji Hoye Turat Mil Jaoon
Ik Pal Ki Talas Mein
Kahet Kabir Suno Bhai Sadho
Mein To Hun Viswas Mein

[Where do you search me?
I am with you
Not in pilgrimage, nor in icons
Neither in solitudes
Not in temples, nor in mosques
Neither in Kaba nor in Kailash
I am with you O man
I am with you

Not in prayers, nor in meditation
Neither in fasting
Not in yogic exercises
Neither in renunciation
Neither in the vital force nor in the body
Not even in the ethereal space
Neither in the womb of Nature
Not in the breath of the breath
Seek earnestly and discover
In but a moment of search
Says Kabir, listen with care
Where your faith is, I am there.]
—Kabir

Chapter 9
CREATING A MEDITATIVE SPACE

Before you begin with your meditation practice, there are a couple of aspects that you must think about. Make an intent to practice regularly. Choosing a space or corner in an undisturbed part of your home (or office) and making it attractive, deciding on a fixed time and duration will support the success of your meditation. This chapter discusses a few things you must consider.

CREATING A SPACE

Establishing an undisturbed place for your meditation routine is exceedingly important, especially if you are new to this practice. It is a signal to the body and mind that you are earnest, which sets the intent for a beginning. Try and look for a corner in your home where you can close the door or a place where nobody will disturb you. I have heard of meditation cushions in bathrooms and restrooms as these sometimes are the most private areas of the house. If you live with a partner, children, or family, it helps to inform the members of the household that you are meditating and would appreciate it if you were not bothered. It makes a lot of sense to use the same place every day and not roam around the house for a new space every so often. This distracts the mind as it has to adjust to new surroundings, sounds, and other distractions before it can settle in.

For some meditators just seeing the meditation space triggers the desire to take a seat. Jon Kabat-Zinn once mentioned, at a retreat I participated in, that we should have a meditation cushion in every room of the house as an inspiration to carry mindfulness and meditation into daily life. Bringing the continuity of meditation into the never-ending inner search for freedom from the known.

Quiet and Undisturbed

Find a place where you can practice without disturbance. Create a small space with room for a chair or a pillow on the floor. If you like to, decorate the space with flowers, an object, or a photograph. You can ignite incense or a candle before you begin. Choose a space that is light and airy and avoids the possibility of anyone passing through. It is important to reserve this space as a peaceful sitting area will remind you of your meditation and can transform the atmosphere of your home in a positive way. You might like to put a sign on the door requesting not to be disturbed during your practice period.

Choice of Seating

Once you have found a space, you should then decide how you would like to sit. If you choose to sit on the floor, you may feel more comfortable using a folded yoga mat or a blanket to protect your knees. It can be helpful to use a meditation cushion, also known as zafu. The zafu should have the right thickness so that your lower body and knees feel supported.

A meditation cushion can help you anchor yourself in the lotus or cross-legged position. Try a height that suits you best and allows your knees and buttocks to settle into a stable three-point position with your spine upright. Keep your back as straight as possible, and your spinal column should be aligned with your neck and head.

If you find the floor uncomfortable for your back, you can sit in a kneeling position with the meditation cushion supporting your buttocks and legs on either side or use a low meditation bench, which allows you to kneel comfortably whilst you fold your lower legs and feet below the bench. A soft surface to rest on is helpful when using the bench.

Alternatively, you can choose a chair with an upright back. The height of the seat should allow your knees to be at a 90-degree angle to the floor. It helps one sit somewhat in front of the chair, to not allow slouching. Should your feet dangle, support them with a flat cushion.

In case being seated is too painful for you, you can lie in a supine position on a blanket with your legs straight or bent at the knees and your arms alongside you. Be aware though, the lying down position invariably leads to sleep, even in experienced meditators. The important point is to be comfortable, relaxed, and stable in whatever position you choose to meditate.

Sometimes it helps to visualise yourself as a water plant, flowing with the current of the water, whilst the bed of the stream, pond, or river remains still and motionless.

Reserve a Fixed Time

If possible, fix a time for your meditation practice. This can either be early in the morning or in the evening before bedtime. Make sure to keep to the same time every day if possible. In case you miss your regular session for whatever reason, it is fine to shift it to another time temporarily. But try and stick to the part of day that works best for you.

Duration

Start your practice gently. Begin with a sequence of three to five minutes for the first two weeks and slowly increase to ten minutes, thereafter, if it feels comfortable. Meditating should make you feel awake, calm, and relaxed. I like to set the duration with a timer. Several apps with timers are available on the internet and they provide a selection of chimes and bells and an occasional guided meditation. My personal favourite is Insight Timer. In case you prefer a vibration to a ringing sound, you can also programme your watch or smartphone to alert you accordingly.

Regularity

Meditation must be practiced regularly. Should you be pressed for time, shorten the normal duration to a few minutes. It is better to practice for a shorter period every day than to meditate for a longer duration sporadically. Regular practice is the key to a deep and insightful meditation practice.

Setting an Intent

Set an intent that you will begin a regular meditation practice to benefit yourself and others. By setting an intent, we tap into our subconscious to support us.

Additional Accessories

To keep you as comfortable as possible, you may want to keep one or two additional cushions and a light blanket in reach. Cushions can be used to support your knees or placed under your head in case you need support. As we sit or lie down for a longer period, our bodies tend to cool down, and it is helpful to cover oneself. In the spirit of self-care, be kind to your body.

THE EXPECTATION OF EXPERIENCES

Meditation is not carried out for an experience. Be accepting of what occurs and what wants to show itself. You may experience sounds, light, a spectrum of colours, a sweet perfume, or sensations (warmth, cold, trembling, the feeling of the body shrinking, becoming larger and larger, your heart opening out wide, etc.) in the body. Sometimes disturbing emotions or images arise. Accept all that appears and let it pass, returning to your object of focus, be it the breath, sensations in the body, or open awareness. Effects reveal themselves unexpectedly and are not linear. Be aware of changes in your attitude and behaviour in relationships, in your coexistence with others, in the dawning of wisdom, and the arising of empathy and compassion.

A Few Cautionary Words About Trauma Sensitivity

In recent years there has been a lot of interest in the area of trauma sensitivity, especially in regard to meditation. The work of David Treleaven, Gregor Mate, and Bessel van der Kolk have revealed that there is a difficult relationship between meditation and trauma. Mindfulness meditation has become extremely popular, particularly in the West with the result that it is offered in several different settings and by teachers with varied backgrounds, ranging from Buddhist communities to clinics, secular programmes, and psychotherapy. It is often promoted as a harmless method for reducing stress and burnout.

Trauma is an increasingly common phenomenon. Research suggests that children are often exposed to significant environmental stressors and adverse situations. In his revolutionary book *The Body Keeps the Score*, Bessel van der Kolk describes that the development of a hyperactive alarm system is promoted by abuse, violence, and threat. It forms a body that gets stuck in the fight, flight, and freeze mode. Additionally, trauma interferes with the brain circuits that involve focusing, flexibility, and being able to stay in emotional control. This constant fear of danger and helplessness causes a continuous secretion of stress hormones in the body, which interfere with the immune system in a drastic manner. To heal, it is important that trauma victims learn to inhabit their bodies and to tolerate feeling what they feel. A wide range of therapeutic interventions are suggested that include various forms of trauma processing, neurofeedback, meditation, and yoga. MBSR has been proven to work in the relief of Post Traumatic Stress Disorder (PTSD), which is often used therapeutically.

What are the effects of sometimes hidden and unknown trauma, which might have occurred in one's childhood and was never talked about? According to the research conducted by Robin Ortiz and Erica M. Sibinga on 'The Role of Mindfulness in Reducing Adverse Effects of Childhood Stress and Trauma', it has been observed that during meditation when the breath is used as an object of focus, the body reacts in an unexpected way. David Treleaven, psychotherapist and worldwide expert on dealing with trauma sensitivity, describes the window of tolerance, which lies between the two extremes of hyper- and hypo-arousal. When in hyper-arousal, we become overly sensitive towards sensations or sounds to the environment and react with high emotional intensity. In hypo-arousal, we may not feel anything; everything is frozen. When we are within this window of tolerance, we can deal with the entire spectrum of our experience. The window of tolerance is connected to our minds. When we are in hyper-arousal, our mind is disorganised, and we find it difficult to concentrate amongst all the stimulation. Sometimes we see disturbing images. When we go into hypo-arousal, our mind and body paralyse, and we cannot think clearly as we become disoriented and lost and have trouble concentrating.

There are a few common symptoms that are observed, should you be experiencing traumatic stress. In the groundbreaking book *Trauma-Sensitive Mindfulness – Practices for Safe and Transformative Healing*, authors David A. Treleaven and Willoughby Britton describe these as:

- Hyperventilation
- Strong perspiration or sweating
- Pale skin
- High or low muscle tone
- Easily startled
- Recognisable disassociation from the body
- Strong mood fluctuations

Some measures that will bring relief are:

- Opening your eyes during the meditation, sometimes it helps to look at an object in your vicinity
- Taking a few long, deep breaths
- Synchronising your breathing with the movements of your hand, opening and closing your fingers on the inbreath and outbreath
- Touching yourself in a compassionate way—put your hand on your belly, your heart, or wherever it feels soothing and comfortable

- Taking a structured break from your meditation—this could be by stretching or walking a few steps back and forth
- Reducing your meditation time
- Holding an object like a stone or bead in your hand

Observe yourself carefully. When you feel comfortable again, you may return to your regular meditation, otherwise it is helpful if you take the advice of a trauma sensitive specialist, psychotherapist, or other qualified person.

IMPLEMENTING A MEDITATION PRACTICE

Topic	Your Answer
When will I meditate?	
What is the minimum length of time that I would like to practice?	
Where will I practice and how do I plan to set it up?	
Which sitting position suits me best? Have I found a chair, a mat, or a cushion for my practice?	
What is my intent?	

PRACTICE MAKES PERFECT!

In *The Power of Habit: Why Do We Do What We Do in Life and Business*, Charles Duhigg mentions that it takes eight weeks of daily practice for a habit to form. Make the intent to meditate once a day for a few minutes. Make copies of the table below and tick the box whenever you complete your meditation in order to keep track of your practice.

Week	Mon	Tues	Wed	Thurs	Fri	Sat	Sun
1							
2							
3							
4							
5							
6							
7							

***

Buddha was once asked, 'What have you gained from meditation?'

He replied, 'Nothing at all! However, let me tell you what I have lost: Anger, anxiety, depression, insecurity, fear of old age and death.'

*There are two kinds of intelligence: one acquired,
as a child in school memorizes facts and concepts
from books and from what the teacher says,
collecting information from the traditional sciences
as well as from the new sciences.*

*With such intelligence you rise in the world.
You get ranked ahead or behind others
in regard to your competence in retaining
information. You stroll with this intelligence
in and out of fields of knowledge, getting always more
marks on your preserving tablets.*

*There is another kind of tablet, one
already completed and preserved inside you.
A spring overflowing its springbox. A freshness
in the centre of the chest. This other intelligence
does not turn yellow or stagnate. It's fluid,
and it doesn't move from outside to inside
through conduits of plumbing-learning.
This second knowing is a fountainhead
from within you, moving out.*
—*Rumi*

Chapter 10
Meditative Postures

*B*efore starting with meditation, it is important to attend to the physical posture of your body. The connection between the posture and the state of mind have been observed for many centuries. A body that slouches will not be overly attentive. Through trial and error, ancient traditions discovered postures that have a positive effect on the collection and concentration of the mind.

This chapter discusses the different seated postures that can be applied whilst meditating. It is important that the spine is erect and vertical to facilitate the flow of air and energy and to connect the earth with the space above. The spine is home to the three energy channels (*nadis*) described in the system of Kundalini yoga, *Ida*, and *Pingala* that wind to the right and left along *sushumna*, located in the spinal cord. At the points of intersection lie the four main nerve plexuses (*chakras*). The seven main chakras begin at the base of the spine (*muladhara chakra*) and end at the crown of the head (*sahasrara chakra*), symbolising the ascent from the physical state (*prakriti*) to the realised state (*samadhi*).

Although meditations like the body scan or tantric sleep (*yoga nidra*) are carried out lying down, meditation is usually carried out seated, whether on a chair or on the floor. It is the tendency of the body to presume that lying down is equivalent to sleep, and it can result in a deep nap (I would like to stress that meditation can be carried out in the lying position).

The following aspects should be taken into consideration when you position your body:

1. Sit with an upright spine and core as this allows your brain to get ample blood and oxygen supply. Sitting straight ensures that you stay awake and alert. Try meditating with a rounded back and watch your frame of mind. An erect backbone enables the breath to flow without obstructing the diaphragm in and out of your lungs. Should your spine involuntarily relax during your practice, simply bring it back to an upright position.

   Try not to rest your back on a wall behind you as the flow of energy within the body is somewhat inhibited. In case you need support to begin with, you can place a bolster or pillow behind your lower back.

2. Place your legs so that they form a stable foundation for the upper body. If you are sitting in a chair, place your feet next to each other, a hand-width apart, so that the soles of the feet make good contact with the floor. Your thighs and calves should make a 90° angle. If necessary, place a cushion below your feet to ensure that this position can be maintained.

   If seated on the floor, keep your pelvis tilted slightly forward and use your back to support the upper part of your body. The seating position is often described as being shaped like a 'V' or a 'tripod', with the buttocks as the base and the knees providing stability on each side. Sit in dignity when you take your seat, 'in your own splendour,' to quote the Ashtavakra Gita or 'like a mountain'.

If seated with your legs crossed (in lotus or half-lotus position), see that your legs are as comfortable as possible. Your left leg should rest inside, towards the body, and the right leg on the outside. Should pain arise, which is normal at the beginning, reposition your body. Be aware of your tailbone as it can get compressed during a longer sitting period. This can be eased by using a zafu.

It is also possible to kneel whilst meditating. Using a meditation mat or placing a soft blanket below the knees eases the pressure on the joints.

Some people also find a meditation bench to be comfortable. These are low benches that allow the placement of the folded legs below the seat of the bench when seated in a kneeling position. The construction of the bench ensures that the spine remains upright.

3. Relax your neck and loosen your shoulders. Pull the shoulder joints up to your ears several times and drop them. The arms should fall loosely on both sides of the torso so that some space remains under the armpits. The shoulders should be straight and at the same height.

4. Place your hands on your knees or your thighs, with your palms down or with your left hand cupping the right hand and thumbs touching. You can also place your fingers in a *mudra*, bringing your thumb and index finger to rest upon each other, your other fingers stretched

out with hands on your knees, facing palm up or palm down.

5. Lower your chin slightly so that the neck is relaxed, and the head can be held straight. Sometimes it helps to position the head if you imagine a thread attaching the crown of your head gently to the ceiling.

6. You can either close your eyes or leave them half-open, letting your somewhat downward gaze gently rest about one to two meters ahead of you. Remember that if you feel overwhelmed during your practice, you can always open your eyes for a while. Sometimes it helps to gaze at an object you like in the room. After a sometime, gently return to keeping your eyes shut.

7. Gently close your lips. If you like you can place the tip of the tongue on the front upper palate. Let your lips be fully relaxed. Loosen the muscles in your cheeks, mouth, around your eyes, and forehead. Smile. A smile releases oxytocin, the hormone of happiness.

8. Breathe through your nose. When practicing mindfulness meditation, it is important to breathe through your nose. Air that we inhale passes through the nasal mucosa, and this stimulates the reflex nerves that control our breathing. When you breathe through the mouth, the breath passes through the nasal mucosa, leading to breathing difficulties and sleep apnea. The air from the nostrils passes via the sinuses that filter, warm, or cool the breath and infuse it with nitric oxide, which helps combat bacteria and viruses in our breath.

Another important aspect is the fact that oxygen is filtered out of the air both on the in- and outbreath. As the area within the nostrils is much smaller, it leads to a slowing down of the airflow, thus allowing more oxygen to be extracted by the lungs. The balanced exchange of carbon dioxide and oxygen enables the blood to maintain its pH value. Losing carbon dioxide too fast, which can occur by breathing out through the mouth, can result in dizziness. In contrast, the increased oxygen intake, which results in breathing through the nostrils, improves our vitality and energy levels.

The nostrils are home to the olfactory system, which is directly connected to the hypothalamus—which is responsible for many autonomic functions like the heartbeat, blood pressure, thirst, sleep cycles, etc. The two nadis, *Ida* and *Pingala*, end in the nostrils.

Perhaps you have noticed that air enters the nose alternately through the left and the right nostrils during the day. Scientific studies have shown that when air flows in through the left nostril the right side of the brain is more dominant, which activates the more creative, emotional part of the brain. Inflow through the right nostril opens the left hemisphere of the brain, which is responsible for analytical, rational, and intellectual mind states. This phenomenon was observed and described by yogis thousands of years ago and the practice of alternate nostril breathing was developed to deliberately balance the physiology of breath-flow.

9. Finally, sitting in stillness, unmoving, grounded, and at ease quietens the mind. As long as the body moves, energies within the body are released, and the senses and the mind cannot find stillness and peace. A few stretching and bending exercises can help to settle the body before sitting down to meditate.

The stillness of the body allows us to get out of the doing mode, and by making the intent not to move, we enable an opening into the interior. We permit ourselves to enter the universe of meditation . . . moving from doing to just being.

All things arise, suffer, change, and eventually pass.

All things arise,
Suffer change,
And pass away.
This is their nature.
When you know this,
Nothing perturbs you,
Nothing hurts you,
You become still.

—Ashtavakra Gita, 11.1

Chapter 11
Meditation Techniques

It is extremely helpful and essential to do some exercises before you sit down to meditate as they help relax the body. The exercises suggested in this chapter include simple stretching and loosening practices based on hatha yoga and breathing exercises based on the yogic method of pranayama.

Mindful hatha yoga is practiced slowly with full attention on the movement. The ancient practice of yoga aims to create a union between body and mind and the individual and universal consciousness.

Mindful movement is a form of meditation in movement as it involves anchoring awareness in the moving body. The posture, too, has an effect on our physical and mental states, thus, bringing our body into specific asanas or positions has effects on our bodies, minds, and emotional condition. Our bodies become more flexible and the heightened awareness of physical posture and what it communicates eventually enables us to change our attitude by changing our postures.

In bringing mindfulness into movement, we focus on the present moment and experience the body, its sensations, thoughts, and emotions that may arise whilst moving our body at a gentle and slow tempo. After each sequence is completed, a felt sense of the body is undertaken. 'What is here now?' is a question we ask ourselves again and again as we connect with the awareness of the present moment.

Mindful movement is carried out with full awareness of each position of the body, every part of that is being moved, experiencing our limits, listening to what the body is telling us, and fully embracing the gentle pace of the movement moment by moment.

Two different forms of mindful movement will be introduced:

- Mindful stretching whilst standing
- Chair yoga

STANDING YOGA

Stand with your feet parallel to each other and approximately shoulder-width apart. The soles of the feet should be well in contact with the floor. Stand upright with your legs slightly bent at the knees and anchor yourself in this pose, which is also called 'Tadasana' or mountain pose. Gently sway from left to right. Experience the sensations in your body. Then sway gently forwards and backwards, again fully aware of what is occurring in the body and mind. Slowly come to a standstill. These gentle movements help you to find your balance in the standing position. Mountain pose is the basis for several movements in the standing position.

If you like you can raise and lower your toes so that your base is firm, like a mountain. Become aware of the sensations in the soles of your feet as you distribute your weight on them.

Your arms should hang loosely on either side of the body and the shoulders relaxed. The neck and head must be balanced. You may like to think of the crown of your head being suspended by a thread from the ceiling.

In the mountain pose you will feel the inner attitude of steadfastness and being rooted to the ground. You are firmly rooted and light and upright at the same time and aware of how securely you are standing here. Fully awake, curious and attentive. Become aware of your breath as it moves in and out of your body and feel your abdomen rise on the inbreath and contract on the outbreath.

Both Arms above the Head

Steady the body and distribute your weight equally on both feet.

Now gently raise your arms, palms facing upwards, towards the ceiling and bring them together, slowly and mindfully, so that your palms are facing each other above your head. Whilst raising your arms be fully aware of the sensations arising in the muscles of the arms, the shoulders, and the upper back. Interlock the fingers and turn the palms upwards.

On an inbreath, gently stretch upward, pushing your palms towards the sky. If you like, you can lift your heels off the ground and stand on your toes. Keep your eyes fixed on a point on the wall in front of you, at the level of your head. This will enable you to keep your balance.

Feel the sensations of the stretch in the muscles and joints of your body, wherever they are arising—in your feet, your legs, your torso, your back, your shoulders, your arms, and your fingers. What are you experiencing during this stretch? Are here any thoughts, emotions, or feelings?

Attend to your breathing and observe any changes in the flow of the breath.

Continue to stretch, finding your limit. In case you have a back, shoulder, or an arm injury, be aware of your own limits or kindly refrain from doing this exercise.

Now, on an outbreath, slowly lower your arms and bring them back to your side. Become aware of the sensations as they drop gently—in your arms, in your hands and fingers, and in your shoulders.

Stand in the starting position with your arms hanging on either side of your body, at ease and at rest.

Take in the after-effects that arise throughout your body after this stretch sequence. Become aware of your breath as you stand and relax.

Raising One Arm and Opposite Heel

On the inhale, raise your left arm, fingers facing the ceiling, and stretch it upwards as if you were picking fruit from a tree. Be fully aware of the sensations that arise throughout the body. Become aware of your breath.

Slowly raise your right heel from the floor to intensify the stretch throughout the body—from the tips of the fingers of your left hand to the toes of the right foot. Stay here for a while. What sensations are you experiencing now?

On an outbreath, release your right heel and gently lower your left arm as you return to the starting position.

Take in the after-effects of the lateral stretch.

Now raise your right arm and repeat the same movements mindfully on the other side, raising your left heel and stretching your right hand upwards, fully aware of the muscles and tendons being pushed to their limits.

Notice what it feels like to be back, standing securely on both feet and how your body is reacting. Take a few breaths.

Bending Sideways

Stand with your feet about a foot-wide apart.

Fix your gaze on a point directly in front of you.

Raise the arms over your head, stretching upwards. Feel the stretch in your body from your toes to your palms.

Now bend to the left from the waist on the inhale. Do not bend forward or backward or twist your torso. Be fully aware of how your body feels in this position.

Breath normally.

On an exhale, gently bring your upper body back to the upright position. On the next inhale, bend your body to the right as you experience the posture on this side of the body.

After a few breaths, on the exhale, slowly bring your arms and torso back to the centre and gently lower your arms to the starting position. Become aware of the sensations arising in the aftermath of this mindful bending exercise.

Shoulder and Arm Rotations

Stand straight with your feet shoulder-width apart and the toes turned slightly out to the side.

Place the tips of your fingers of both hands on your shoulders, with the elbows pointing sideways. This is the starting position.

Rotate the shoulders gently in clockwise direction. Whilst rotating raise the elbows upwards, then bring them in front of the body, as far as they will go, then rotate them backward as if you were trying to draw the shoulder blades together and raise them upwards again.

Roll your shoulders through these positions approximately five times, feeling the sensations arising in this movement in the upper back, the torso, and the shoulders.

Change the direction to anticlockwise, starting with moving your elbows to the back of the body, upwards, towards the front and finally downwards. Repeat about five times.

Gently lower your arms and bring them back to rest on either side of your body. Feel the after-effects of this exercise.

Remain still for a while and embrace the sensations arising in your body.

(Source: Adapted from the mindful yoga movements in the MBSR programme)

CHAIR YOGA

These exercises can be done seated in a normal office chair. Often, we become stiff and lose flexibility due to long hours of sitting in front of a computer screen or at a desk. These simple stretching and loosening exercises will help you to open your joints, strengthen your back and abdomen muscles, and improve flexibility. Performed before meditation, they relax the body, reducing sensations and unwanted movement whilst sitting in stillness.

Hands Raised Pose

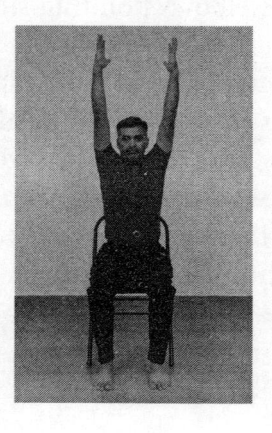

Sit straight on a chair, with your arms are hanging loosely on either side of your body.

On an inhale, raise both your arms slowly towards the ceiling, initially at 180 degrees and then finally above your head.

Maintain a stable upper body posture with the shoulders relaxed and rib cage sitting naturally. Anchor your sitting bones in your chair and reach up from there. Then slowly bring them back to the starting position.

Synchronise your breath with your movements, inhaling when you raise your arms and exhaling when you lower your arms.

Repeat five or ten times.

Forward Spinal Twist

Sit on the chair with an upright spine and your feet approximately a foot apart.

Bend forward and bring your left fingertips to the floor in the centre between both your feet.

Simultaneously open your chest as you twist to the right on an inhale, raising your right arm towards the ceiling, with your palm facing to the left. Bring your gaze to the ceiling. This is the extended side angle pose. Hold for several breaths. Bring the right arm down on an exhale and raise the left arm from the floor. Lower both arms to rest on either side of your body.

If your left hand cannot reach the floor, help yourself by placing a yoga block or thick book on the floor and use this for support, or bring your hand to your left knee instead and twist from there.

Repeat this exercise on the other side by lowering your right arm to the floor and bringing your left arm up.

Repeat on each side for five or ten times.

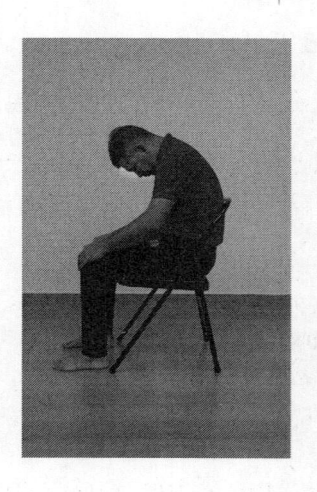

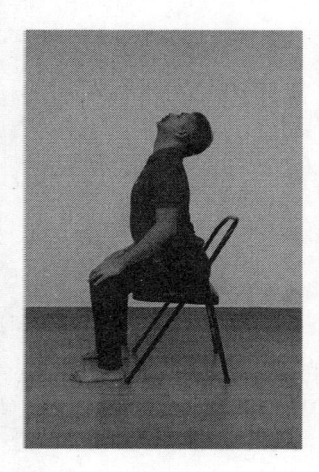

Cat and Cow Stretch

Sit on a chair with the spine upright and both feet on the floor. Place your hands on your knees or on the top of your thighs.

On an inhale, arch your spine and roll your shoulders back and down, bringing your shoulder blades closer to each other on your back. This is the cow position. Let your head drop behind with ease.

On an exhale, round and hunch your spine and drop your chin to your chest, letting your shoulders and head come forward. This is the cat position.

Continue moving between cow on inhalation and cat on exhalation for five to ten breaths.

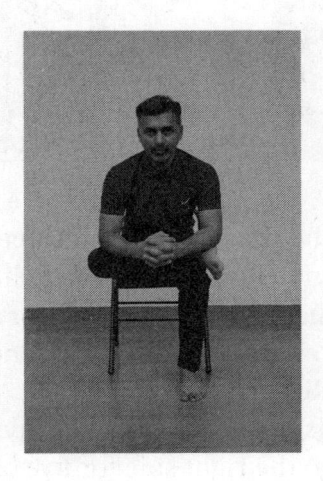

Hip Opener

Sit on the chair facing forward, feet about a foot apart.

Bring your right ankle to rest on your left thigh, keeping the right knee aligned with your right ankle as much as possible. Hold this chair hip opener for three to five breaths.

You may bend forward to intensify the stretch by placing the right elbow on the right knee and pressing the right knee down. Please do this only if you are comfortable. Repeat with the left leg.

Repeat on both sides five to ten times.

Spinal Twist (Ardha Matsyendrasana)

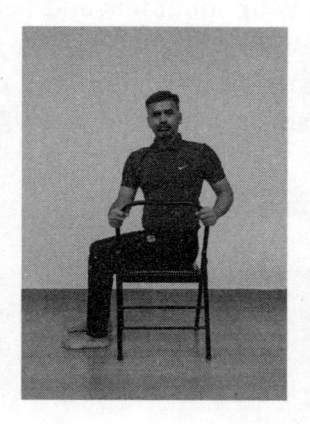

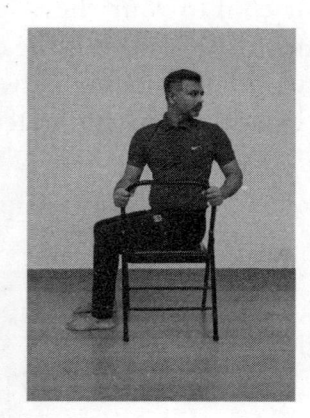

Sit sideways on the chair, facing to the left.

Twist your torso towards the left, holding onto the backrest of the chair with both hands for a spinal twist.

Lengthen your spine on each inhale and twist to the left on each exhale. Repeat for five breaths.

Move your legs around to the right side of the chair and repeat the twist to the right side for five breaths.

Lateral Spine Stretch

Sit forward at the edge of the chair.

Place your feet about 30 cm apart, turning the feet forty-five degrees outwards so that the knees and toes are in one line.

Place the right forearm on the centre of the right thigh, allowing the spine to lean on the right side.

Raise your left arm and bring the upper arm close to the left ear.

Start stretching from the left fingertips down to the waist. Hold there for five breaths.

Repeat on the other side.

Hugging Yourself or Opening and Closing Your Arms Horizontally

Make yourself comfortable on a chair with an upright spine and your feet approximately 10 cm apart.

Keep your arms hanging on either side to begin with.

On the inbreath, gently raise both arms upwards, parallel to the floor.

On the outbreath wrap your arms around your chest, as if you were cuddling a child.

On the inbreath open the arms out wide.

On the outbreath hug yourself once more by bringing your arms across your chest, this time with the other arm below.

Then on the outbreath open your arms wide again.

Then gently lower the arms into the starting position.

Repeat for five times on each side, hugging yourself whilst synchronising your movements with the breath.

Be totally aware of and one with your breath flow in and out of the body.

To conclude, shake your arms out.

No one has form without breath, Consequently, breath and form must be accomplished together. Isn't this evident?
—*Master Great Nothing of Sung-Shan,*
Taoist Canon on breathing

Chapter 12
BREATHING EXERCISES

Although meditations often use the breath as an object of attention for focus, breathing exercises open up the breath pathways, unblock airway passages, and calm and stabilise the mind. This enables an easy entry into the practice of meditation.

The process of breathing, like our heartbeat, is inseparable from life and consciousness itself. From the second we are born till our last breath, the process of breathing is a permanent, often an unnoticed companion. Did you know that the breath flows in and out of the body about 11,000 times a day, in total 22,000 times? Respiration is the basis of every form of life—from the plant kingdom to the birds, mammals, fish, and single-celled creatures.

In many cultures the breath is considered sacred. *Psyche pneuma* is the Greek translation for 'soul/spirit/breath'. In Latin, *anima spiritus* means 'breath/soul'. In Japanese *ki* stands for 'air/spirit' and in Chinese the character for breath *hsi* is made up of three characters that denote 'of the conscious self or heart'. In Sanskrit, *prana* is equivalent to a life force that is extinguished at death. Donna Farhi, in her book *The Breathing Book*, describes the breath as a force that runs through the mind, body, and spirit like a river running through a dry valley giving sustenance to everything in its course.

Ancient wisdom traditions such as Taoism and yoga and the medical sciences of Ayurveda, Tibet, and China have described the connection between breathing and the state of our body and mind. Recently, especially in the aftermath of Covid-19, there has been a steep rise in publications on the power of breathing.

YOUR LUNGS, THE RIB CAGE AND THE DIAPHRAGM

Your lungs are in a protective enclosure of the ribs and the sternum. They reach from the top of the collarbones down to the tenth thoracis vertebra in your spine. You can visualise the bottom of your lungs if you place your hands approximately 10 cm above your waist. The rib cage is attached to the breastbone in the front of the body and to the spine at the back and is made of movable parts that enable it to expand and contract effortlessly whilst breathing. This is also enabled by the intercostal muscles between the ribs and the diaphragm, which forms the barrier towards the other organs of the body. You can imagine the diaphragm as large dome-shaped muscle that lies in the chest and radiates out from there to either side, connected by muscles and tendons.

When the diaphragm moves, all our organs are massaged and bathed in fresh oxygen and blood. Breathing stimulates the entire body, giving us a sense of well-being and health. The diaphragm is lowered on the inhale and displaces the organs in the belly, leading to the abdomen to expand gently. Inspiration occurs by the large space in the chest this movement triggers, thereby lowering the pressure in the chest. The difference in pressure to the atmosphere causes air to flow into the body, to balance this pressure. When we exhale, the diaphragm relaxes and returns upwards, compressing the air in the chest and allowing it to flow out of the body. In addition to moving upwards and downwards, the diaphragm also broadens and moves outwards. Therefore, the expansion and contraction of the diaphragm must not be restricted to enable a free flow of air during inspiration and expiration.

The following four breathing exercises are based on the science of pranayama, one of the eight branches of yoga. They are easy to practice and allow your breath to settle gently, stilling your mind, as you sit down for meditation.

NATURAL BREATHING

This is a simple technique that introduces you to your respiratory system and the breathing space. Natural breathing slows down the respiratory rate and establishes a more relaxed rhythm, thus, soothing the body.

Instructions

Sit in a comfortable position on a chair with your feet about 15 cm apart, an upright spine, and relaxed shoulders and arms. If you prefer, you can also lie on your back. Relax your entire body.

Observe the natural and spontaneous breathing process as your breath flows rhythmically in and out of your body.

Become aware of the breath flowing in and out of your nostrils.

Feel the breath flowing in and out at the back of your mouth and palate.

Bring your awareness to your throat and feel the breath flowing through it.

Now move your awareness to the chest and feel the flow of the breath into the trachea and bronchial tubes.

Then, feel the breath flowing into your lungs, becoming aware of the lungs expanding and relaxing on the inbreath and outbreath.

Move your attention to the ribcage and observe the expansion and relaxation of this area.

Now attend to the abdomen and feel it move upward on the inbreath and downward on the outbreath as the diaphragm broadens whilst breathing in and relaxes whilst breathing out.

Finally, become aware of the entire breathing process from the nostrils to the abdomen and continue observing it for a while. Feel your entire body breathing, the front, the back, and the sides of the body as you massage your internal organs with each breath.

Bring the awareness back to observing the physical body as a whole. Open your eyes to conclude this breathing exercise.

THREE-PART BREATHING

The three-part breathing practice combines abdominal, thoracic, and clavicular breathing. It is used to maximise inhalation and exhalation.

Abdominal Breathing

Abdominal breathing is the most natural and efficient way to breathe. However, due to tension, stress, and bad posture, it is often forgotten. Once this technique becomes part of one's daily life, there is great improvement in the state of physical and mental health and well-being.

Instructions

Sit in a chair or in a meditative posture on the floor. Relax your entire body.

Place your right hand on the abdomen, just above the navel, and your left hand over the centre of the chest.

Alternately, you can form the fingers of your hands into a *mudra* or gesture, which activates the meridians and directs energy throughout the body, restoring the flow of energy. The mudra used during abdominal breathing is called the 'chin mudra'. Lightly touch the tip of your thumb with the tip of your index finger to form a circle, keeping the other fingers straight but relaxed. Do this with both the right and left hands. The chin mudra activates the diaphragm, making for deep stomach breathing as the diaphragm pushes out the internal organs during inhalation.

Inhale whilst expanding the abdomen and feel your right hand move upwards. At the end of the inhalation, the diaphragm will be compressing the abdomen and the navel will be at its highest point.

Exhale whilst the abdomen relaxes, feeling your hand move downwards. On exhalation, the diaphragm moves upward, and the abdomen moves downward. In the end, the abdomen will be contracted, and the navel is compressed towards the spine.

Repeat this process of inhalation and exhalation for ten rounds, connecting to your abdomen as you breathe.

Thoracic Breathing

Thoracic breathing uses the middle lobes of the lungs by expanding and contracting the ribcage. It is often associated with stress and tension and with physical exercise and exertion.

Instructions

Sit in a meditation posture or on a chair and or lie on your back. Relax the entire body.

If you like you can place your fingers on each hand in the 'chinmaya mudra'. In this mudra, the thumb and forefinger are the same as they are in the chin mudra. The only difference is that the other three fingers are curled into the palm. Gently rest the hands palm down on the middle of your thighs. This mudra activates the ribs, causing them to expand sideways on inhalation.

Maintain unbroken awareness of the natural breath for some time, focusing on the chest.

Now feel your ribcage expanding and rising slightly as you inhale, becoming aware of the air moving into this area.

As you exhale, feel your chest dropping, your ribs contracting, and the air leaving your body through the nostrils.

Breathe in and out by focusing your attention on the ribcage and its gentle movement on the inhale and exhale.

Repeat for ten breath cycles, connecting to your chest area as you breathe.

Clavicular Breathing

Clavicular breathing is the final stage of the breath process. It occurs after the thoracic inhalation has been completed. In clavicular breathing, the air is drawn into the chest by the raising of the upper ribcage and the collarbone (clavicles), and the simultaneous contraction of the abdomen during inhalation. Normally, clavicular breathing occurs only during extreme physical exertion.

Instructions

Sit in a chair or lie down on your back on a mat.

Relax your entire body and breathe naturally through your nose.

If you wish, you can place your hands in 'adi mudra' by folding the thumb into the palm of your hand, touching the base of the small finger. The other fingers are folded over the thumb, making a fist. Gently place the hands palm down on the middle of your thighs. The adi mudra stimulates the pectoral muscles, making the chest expand upwards on inhalation.

Now feel your upper ribcage and collarbone expanding and rising slightly as you inhale, becoming aware of the air moving into this area.

As you exhale, feel your upper ribcage and collarbone falling. This area contracts slightly and the air leaves your body through the nostrils.

Breathe in and out by focusing your attention on the upper ribcage and collarbone and their gentle movement on both the inhalation and exhalation.

Repeat for ten breath cycles.

ALTERNATE NOSTRIL BREATHING

In this breathing exercise, the breath is alternately breathed through the left and the right nostrils. There are different forms of alternate nostril breathing. The following instructions describe a simple but effective method for this practice.

Hand Position

Before we begin this exercise, we have to learn the specific hand position used. This position, also called Vishnu mudra, regulates the flow of breath between the left and the right nostrils. Usually, the right hand is used. If you feel more comfortable, you can use your left hand.

Open your right hand and bend the index and middle finger. Keep the ring finger upright and either slightly bend your little finger or keep it as upright as possible. Do not strain your hand, just make sure to keep the thumb and ring finger mobile.

During alternate nostril breathing, the right hand is placed in front of the face. The thumb is above the right nostril and the ring finger is above the left nostril. These two digits control the flow of the breath in the nostrils by alternately pressing on one nostril, blocking the flow of breath, and then the other.

Instructions

Sit in a comfortable meditation posture or in a chair, keeping your spine upright and your head straight. Relax your body. Close your eyes.

Begin by breathing in and out slowly and gently for a few minutes, stabilising and centring your breath.

Adopt the hand position with your right hand and place your left hand on your knee. Close your right nostril with your thumb.

Inhale through the left nostril slowly and gently and count till three as you do so.

Close the left nostril, release your thumb from the right nostril, and exhale slowly and softly to the count of five, gently expelling all the air from your lungs through the nostril.

Keeping your ring finger on the left nostril, inhale from the right nostril to the count of three.

Release the ring finger and breath out from your left nostril, pressing your right nostril gently with your thumb. Count to five whilst exhaling.

This is one round of alternate nostril breathing.

Continue this process for five or ten rounds, making sure that there is no sound as the air passes through the nostrils.

Should you feel more comfortable with another rhythm, feel free to adapt a more suitable one. The length of the exhalation should be longer than that of the inhalation as this increases the effect of relaxation.

This technique increases awareness of and sensitivity to the breath in the nostrils. Minor blockages are removed and the flow of breath in the nostrils balances itself. Breathing through the left nostril tends to activate the right hemisphere of the brain, breathing through the right nostril activates the left hemisphere. Balanced breathing calms and balances vital energies.

HUMMING BEE BREATH

Humming bee breath or bhramari pranayama is named after the Hindu goddess Bhramari, the goddess of bees. The name is fitting as the light humming sound of the bhramari breath alludes to the buzzing sound that bees' wings make. This simple breath practice has numerous applications that can have profound effects on the mind and body.

Instructions

Sit in a comfortable meditation position, preferably on the floor. If this is not possible you can sit in a chair. Rest your hands on your knees if seated in a crossed leg or kneeling position.

Relax the whole body and close your eyes.

Your lips should remain closed, with the teeth slightly separated during this practice, allowing the vibration of sound to be heard and felt.

Raise your arms sideways, bending your arms at the elbows and bring your hands to your ears. Use your index finger to gently close your ears.

Alternately, you can close your ears with your thumbs and gently rest the four fingers of your hands on your eyes.

Inhale through your nostrils. Exhale through your nose whilst making a steady humming sound like that of a bee.

The humming sound should be smooth, controlled, even, and continuous for the duration of the exhalation. It could make the skull reverberate. Your fingers should feel the vibrations of the sound.

At the end of the exhalation, keep your hands steady on your ears or return them to your knees, to raise them again for the second round.

Both inhalation and exhalation should be rhythmic and controlled.

Repeat this procedure for five rounds.

For he, who has gained control over his breath, shall also gain control over the activities of the mind. The reverse is also true. For he, whose mind is in control, also controls the breath. The mind masters the senses, and the breath masters the mind.

—*Hatha Yoga Pradipika*

Chapter 13

COMMON OBSTACLES IN MEDITATION

*I*ntegrating meditation into daily life is often a challenging task. Meditation can be frustrating, boring, or can come across as a waste of time. It can be difficult to fit it into a busy schedule unless you consciously allot a slot during the day. Especially when you start a meditation practice, sitting still for long periods can cause pain or discomfort in the body.

It is perfectly normal for problems to arise during meditation. We all at some point in our lives learn a new skill. Whether it's cycling or playing an instrument, a new language, the process of learning requires practise and, above all, patience.

Accept the obstacles that arise and see them as a learning opportunity to understand yourself better. Many students of meditation encounter hinderances, some of which I have put together in this chapter. Perhaps you, too, will recognise yourself in one or the other. I will explain the most important obstacles and give you simple tips on how to deal with them in the best way possible. These tips are not new; they have been observed and described in many ancient traditions.

Meditation is not linear. Its effects and insights dawn unexpectedly. The most important thing is to not lose heart and give up.

LACK OF TIME

'I don't have time to meditate' is one of the most common arguments by a beginner. The household, the children, and other tasks that take precedence are common excuses that we make to justify our behaviour. A well-known Zen story describes a familiar situation:

> A forest worker was painstakingly sawing a large pile of wood and was making slow progress. A few hikers passed by and observed him for a while, watching him shout and curse whilst sweating profusely. The passers-by asked the woodcutter why he did not sharpen his saw. He shook his head indignantly and answered, 'Can't you see the amount of work I have? I do not have the time to sharpen my saw. I have to saw!'

Make an intent to meditate and see it as an important enrichment of your life. Then you will make time for your practice. Meditate for a few minutes to begin with, and slowly increase the duration. Even three minutes is enough for a beginner.

Be sure to meditate regularly at a fixed time in the morning or in the evening. Just make sure to set aside the time. If you cannot fix a time, then meditate whenever you can once a day, leaving the hard and fast rule aside.

LACK OF SPACE

'I don't have a quiet place to sit in,' is another excuse I often hear. The children, the traffic noise, the neighbours, the dog barking . . .

Find a small place in a corner where you can sit comfortably on a cushion on the floor or in a straight-backed chair. Try to sit in the same place every day. At the workplace, this can be your office chair or, if possible, a break room where you will not be disturbed. Avoid passageways, thoroughfares, or meeting rooms.

Try hanging a handwritten notice requesting not to be disturbed.

PHYSICAL PAIN OR DISCOMFORT

'My leg has fallen asleep,' 'It is itching,' 'I cannot stand the pain anymore,' 'Will I ever be able to walk again?'

Aches and pains are quite natural when the body sits still for a longer time. Common physical sensations are stiffness, throbbing, itching, stinging, numbness, pain, or other feelings of discomfort. Inconvenience can be a great teacher. But do I try to accept these sensations and accept them for the moment, or do I resist them and turn away?

Watch out how your mind responds to physical difficulties. Is there rejection or avoidance involved? Is there acceptance for the sensation? The key is to consciously perceive the actual sensation and the thoughts and feelings that arise. You will notice that if you observe the sensation for a while, it waxes and wanes. You will find that the pain eventually dissolves and your attitude to discomfort changes as well.

Below are a few tips on dealing with discomfort:

- Knee pain – Support your knees on either side with a small soft pillow to release the pressure.
- Backache – Keep a soft pillow behind your lower back to ease the tension. If you are sitting on a chair, place a small flat cushion between the curve of your back and the backrest of the chair.
- Leg pain – Stretch your leg out and fold it back again once the pain is relieved. If you are sitting

in a chair, raise your leg and place it on stool in front of you.

Mindful movement – Before you sit down to meditate, it is helpful to do a few mindful exercises (see Chapters 10 & 11). This warms up the body, relaxes the muscles, and prevents discomfort.

RESTLESSNESS AND INTERNAL DISTRACTIONS

A body that is not used to sitting or lying still is often faced with unwanted movement or sensations that can distract the attention from the object of meditation. The resulting restlessness of the body can additionally be disturbed by different kinds of internal distractions. These can be triggered by a sense organ (smell or hearing) or by a reaction to an external distraction. A further internal distraction is the thought flow produced by the mind.

We are accustomed to being in 'doing mode' since our childhood and the forever-active mind rebels when it is forced to linger in 'being mode', in doing nothing. Just as our body is home to all kinds of sensations, our mind constantly produces thoughts. Thoughts come in all forms and arise as to-do lists, images, plans, mind-wanderings, thoughts of the past and speculations of the future and many others. This is perfectly normal.

Observe the distractions with interest. Do not cling to a distraction and allow thought-castles to enmesh your mind. Let the distraction pass, like a cloud in the sky, and bring your attention back to your point of focus—the breath, the body, etc.

Begin your practice with mindful movement or yoga. Gentle exercises help calm the body and mind as well as adjust them to a period of silence.

BOREDOM AND DISLIKE

Despite beginning a meditation practice with great enthusiasm, sometimes the false perception creeps in that it is all a sheer waste of time. Our fast-paced lifestyles and society are a constant source of distraction. All kinds of stimuli vie for our attention. The more conditioned we are to responding instantly to any form of distraction, the easier it is that a lack thereof produces the feeling of boredom.

Dislike is a negative affliction created by the mind when it begins to categorise. Boredom and dislike can manifest themselves especially at the beginning of your meditation practice. Be careful with boredom because it can lead you to stop meditating.

These are some ways you can deal with boredom and distraction during meditation:

- Meet these feelings with curiosity and acceptance. Be aware that boredom and dislike dissolve by themselves.
- Become aware of the thoughts that relate to boredom and do not grasp on to them.
- Observe your body and watch where boredom arises and what it does with the body.
- Observe your boredom. Take an outside perspective and watch the boredom arise within you as separate from yourself.
- Bring your attention back to your breath and observe what happens to this feeling of boredom.

SLEEPINESS OR DROWSINESS

'I fell asleep again!' 'Did I snore?' Many of my students struggle with sleepiness when they start meditating. As soon as our hectic mind calms down, we feel drowsiness setting in. This happens especially when we meditate in a lying down position but also whilst sitting. Suddenly, you might jerk as your head drops down to your chest or your body moves to one side. Sleepiness is a perfectly natural occurrence.

Mindfulness makes us more alert and conscious, but the mind sometimes wants to avoid getting into this state of pure awareness. Another factor is, we are often physically tired by our lifestyle. The moment we become still, the body takes its chance to relax and release all tension, often resulting in sleep. If you fall asleep, do not make a big deal of it.

- A common remedy is to open your eyes and gaze upwards towards the ceiling a few times; then return to your usual eye position.
- Try and meditate with open or half-open eyes. Even though this may seem a bit uncomfortable to begin with, keeping your eyes open during meditation helps you remain alert and awake. Some meditation traditions require you to sit with eyes open. This practice trains the mind to remain still despite visual distractions that may be present.
- Do some mindful movement before sitting down to meditate—yoga, standing postures, or mindful walking—to prepare the body for longer spells of sitting.

- Make sure that you have slept enough as it prevents drowsiness during meditation.
- Limit your food intake before meditating—a small snack or drink of water should suffice instead of taking a heavy meal as the latter will cause your energies to be directed towards digestion.
- Observe the best time of day for your practice and try to meditate at different times of the day. For some, morning is the best time; for others, evening is more conducive.

NON-PERFECTION

There is no such thing as a perfect meditation practice. 'Am I doing this correctly?', 'This works for others, but not for me!', 'How do I know whether my practice is right?' are some queries that I often hear. In the practice of mindfulness, there is nothing to be perfect at, nothing to achieve, nowhere to go, and nothing to compete against. Remain in touch with yourself and your breath from moment to moment. All you have to do is accept each session as it is and not look for errors. Mindfulness is an open and wide field and the acceptance of whatever is occurring is part of the practice.

EXPECTING 'EVENTS' OR 'EXPERIENCES'

'I did not experience anything today' or 'What experiences are waiting for me?' are typical questions that arise. Our minds see meditation as another experience, like all the experiences we have in our distracted world. Meditation is by no means entertainment in the worldly sense and definitely not an event. Meditation has a higher goal beyond experiencing.

- Whilst meditating, do not look out for experiences. The path is the goal, and it is new each time, like every moment.
- Go into each session with an open mind and no goal or plan.
- If sitting in silence is difficult, you can do a guided meditation. Numerous apps, online guided meditations, or audios are available. Several excellent teachers have recorded guided meditations.

DIFFICULT EMOTIONS

During meditation, thoughts, sensations, and emotions appear on the screen of awareness. When difficult emotions arise, it is important not to build resistance against them. Allow the emotions to be there and observe them dissolve after a while, without allowing the mind to feed them with thoughts. Just let them be.

A difficult emotion usually has a deeper message. By remaining with the emotion, recognising, and perhaps labelling it and then accepting the emotion, a transformation occurs, which allows the cause to gently come to the fore. Like in a big pot some emotions rise, are seen, and if not pushed away, they dissolve. The process heals difficult emotions by triggering an inner understanding.

THE MONKEY MIND

Many practitioners report an overactive thought process or a carousel of thoughts as soon as they sit down in silence for meditation. In Buddhism, the hyperactive mind is called the 'monkey mind'. You can imagine it like this—the monkey mind prefers to jump from tree to tree, or from branch to branch, and never comes to rest. The monkey mind represents our thoughts or our attention.

Our mind tends to wander, create stories, and simply produce thoughts. Each thought has a relatively short span when observed carefully. By not clinging on to it, thoughts pass, like dry leaves in the wind or like the clouds in the sky. The key is to acknowledge them and bring your attention back to what you have set your intention on—be it the breath, the body, or whatever is present. This process may repeat itself several times. The awareness of a distraction is an act of mindfulness . . . a 'magic moment'.

- Try and observe your monkey mind when you start your meditation practice. For many, silence is unpleasant because the world around us is loud and full of distractions. Watch your thoughts come and go and become a distanced observer.
- Note that burgeoning thoughts often tend to result in stories. An example could be: 'I'll go home soon . . . my daughter is waiting for dinner . . . what do I cook today . . . perhaps spaghetti bolognese . . . can't remember whether there is enough spaghetti . . . must go to the supermarket . . . for how long it is open today . . .' And suddenly we find ourselves in the midst of a cascade of thoughts, far away from our original intention of observing the breath. Be aware of the creative power of your storytelling mind.
- Consciously be aware of the wandering mind and bring your attention back again and again gently. At some point, the mind will have enough

of being rebuked, thus reducing the thoughts, or no longer distracting you.
- Lastly, try to reduce an over-stimulation of your senses before you sit down to meditate.

Remember, thoughts are not facts even if they like to think they are.

ARROGANCE

A final note on a disruptive factor that can come up, arrogance, which I sometimes observe in practitioners of meditation. Meditators are not in any way 'better' people, but individuals who train their minds and delve deep into the wisdom of life. See yourself as someone lucky to be able to pursue this subject and be aware that true wisdom emerges from the heart.

Should a feeling of arrogance occur, recognise it, do not dwell on it, and release it.

*The mind is like a monkey swinging from branch to branch through a forest. In order not to lose sight of the monkey by some sudden movement, we must watch the monkey constantly and even be one with it. Mind contemplating mind is like an object and its shadow—the object cannot shake the shadow off. The two are one. Wherever the mind goes, it still lies in the harness of the mind . . .
Once the mind is directly and continually aware of itself, it is no longer like a monkey.*

—Thich Nhat Hanh, *The Miracle of Mindfulness*

Chapter 14
Living Mindfully

*I*nformal mindfulness practice takes place in the moment during which you perform your routine daily activities. By making presence, curiosity, wakefulness, and awareness a part of every moment of your life, mindfulness becomes a way of living and being. For instance, being always present with your loved ones and not distracted by thoughts about work. Or whilst at a meal, by putting your smartphone and other sources of distraction away and enjoying the food with all your senses. Keep your default mode, your wandering mind, and multitasking aside, and just be fully present at whatever you are doing.

Below are a few ways to make mindfulness a way of life.

WAKING UP WITH MINDFULNESS

Try to incorporate mindfulness into your morning routine, making both the formal practice of meditating and the informal practice of living mindfully a part of your everyday life.

- A mindful morning begins when you wake up and you start the day with some mindful breaths and a smile on your face, looking forward to what awaits you today.
- You may stand up and go to the window and look for a few minutes into the garden or onto

the street. Watching attentively which sounds, smells, and visual stimuli are perceptible.
- Stretch your muscles and do some mindful movements, fully aware of your body moving, breathing, expanding, and contracting.
- You may want to sit down for a mindfulness meditation.
- Go to the kitchen mindfully and make yourself a cup of tea or coffee, enjoying the scent and sounds of the water boiling in the kettle or the coffee brewing.
- Take a shower and be aware whilst the water flows onto your skin, perhaps following the drop to its point of origin, into the water tank, pipes, lake, or mountain stream.

MINDFUL COMMUNICATION

When you talk to your partner, children, or friends, try to be present. Mindful communication means that you listen with full attention. This can be unpleasant at first as we are used to agreeing, butting in, completing the other's sentences, or sharing similar experiences. Do not give in to the impulse. Always draw your attention back to the person you are with, using the opposite as an anchor. When listening deeply, listen to the tone of the voice and be attentive to non-verbal communication. Mindful speaking is limited to communicating the essential aspects of a conversation. Think about what you say and when, the choice of words, and whether the situation is appropriate. Sometimes, communicating mindfully means choosing silence.

MINDFUL WALKING

The next time you go for a walk, make yourself fully aware of the fact that you are walking. Feel the connection to the ground or the earth below your feet and perceive the breeze on your skin. Hear the birds chirping, consciously inhale the scents of the forest, the meadow, the sea, or the flowers. Feel the moss, the tree bark, or the stones along the path as you transform your walk into a mindful feast of the senses. Try to keep your attention on the experience. If your thoughts diverge, direct your attention back to the full experience of walking, step-by-step, moment by moment.

MINDFUL DRIVING

Take in the car, the contact to the seat below and behind you, the texture of the seat covers, the steering wheel beneath your hands and the fact that you are embarking on a journey, however short or long.

Before you start driving take a minute to focus on your breath. Relax your body and release all the tension in your body—your shoulders, your upper and lower back, your arms, and if necessary, your stomach as well. Allow all the tension to flow out of your body whenever you exhale, releasing and relaxing on the outbreath.

Perhaps you can opt not to turn on your radio to be fully aware of yourself whilst driving and to be in silence with yourself.

When you stop at a signal, use the time to focus on your breath and observe your thought flow, emotions, and the sensations arising in your body.

Try to watch your emotions whilst driving. If someone cuts you, breaks suddenly or drives rashly, observe the emotions and reactions that spontaneously arise.

Remember the space between trigger and reaction and your active choice to stay calm and in equanimity.

Try driving somewhat slower than usual if you are on a freeway. Observe what this does to your feelings and sensations.

Be mindful of pedestrians, cyclists, and other players in your circle of attention as you consciously switch off your default mode and switch on awareness in the present.

MINDFUL BREAKS

Make sure to take conscious breaks during the day to really relax throughout the day. They could be a few minutes long during which you observe your thought flow, your breath, and your bodily sensations.

Use cues in your environment as a reminder to centre yourself, like the phone ringing, a red light, a bell, or programme a regular alarm on your phone.

Use a break to breathe deeply for the length of three to five breaths, thereby changing the mode of your brain from doing to being.

MINDFUL EATING

Eating mindfully stimulates all the five senses and sensory organs, allowing us to become fully aware of the visual, auditory, taste, olfactory, and somatosensory aspects of the food. By observing your thought and emotional reactions when you sit down for a meal, taking in the plate, the colours, and all the elements in front of you, the act of eating takes on a different dimension.

Preparing and cooking a meal mindfully prolongs the entire process. By being fully aware whilst peeling and cleaning the ingredients until the dish is steaming on the stove, mindfulness becomes an art of living.

During and after a mindful meal your digestion and long-term satiety are stimulated. Make eating an occasional mindful meal a part of your food hygiene.

MINDFULNESS AT THE WORKPLACE

Your workplace and attitude towards work can be infused with awareness and mindfulness, leading you to become more focused, clearer, and compassionate towards your colleagues.

1. Start your working day at your desk with a pause. Set your intent to bring a mindful, present way of working to your day. You may like to take three deep breaths.
2. Avoid multitasking as the brain can only focus on one activity at a time. So doing things simultaneously leads to fatigue, more mistakes, lack of concentration, and distraction. Take up one task after the other and unless it is unavoidable, do not allow yourself to be interrupted.
3. Make a clear intent that you will be present for most of your working day. We often tend to be in the past or in the future. Keep bringing your mind to the report or task you are working on and do not permit your mind to take you on a flight of fantasy.
4. Slow down to speed up. This could seem a bit counter-intuitive as by stopping or slowing down, you can become more efficient, productive, happy, resilient, and healthy at work. Rushing around and hastily making decisions leads to bad choices and drains your energy. By slowing

down, you focus on listening, take a break, walk with control rather than run, and generally take your time when at work. Leaders and people who are effective slow down, think, and reflect to make appropriate decisions and actions, in that by slowing down they speed up.

5. Accept what cannot be changed. Being mindful is to accept yourself, whatever is occurring and the present moment, as it is. Acceptance is an acknowledgement of how things are without trying to change them and is not the same as giving up or resigning yourself to fate (which is passive). If you can change a situation, then do so; if you fail, then learn to accept it with grace.

6. Be grateful and show gratitude for the work you have, the colleagues you work with, your team, and your clients. A simple thank you or act of kindness every day will make you feel happier and more satisfied. Start a gratitude journal or just remember the unexpected, pleasant experiences during the day before you go to sleep at night.

7. Avoid the brain's negativity trap. Our brains are programmed to remember threatening, negative impressions. Instead of dwelling on something that's gone wrong, remind yourself of things that have gone successfully. The negativity bias can make us adopt an excessively negative and unbalanced way of thinking. Keep seeing and bringing in the positive in your day. You might like to write down five positive things that you saw, heard, or encountered. Just a memory of them produces positive pathways in the brain and promotes a positive outlook and attitude.

8. Apply a beginner's mind whenever you do something new or meet someone and have an open mindset. Challenge the way you deal with problems. Try and see a bigger picture, allow your world to become bigger by seeing with the eyes of a child. Leave your conditioned habits and behaviours behind you. Every moment is fresh with new potential.

ENDING THE DAY WITH CARE

When you get home, take a moment to make a conscious decision to being fully aware of arriving back. Non-conceptual activities are wonderfully suited to practice mindfulness. Try to be conscious when you iron, mow the lawn, do homework with the children, or other household chores. Your brain switches from conceptual to experiential mode.

- Cooking is a perfect opportunity to practice mindfulness. Prepare your meal with love and attention. Your family will taste it!
- Mindful conversations with your family or partner lead to better understanding and compassion. Listen deeply when someone tells you something about their day. Observe how much of what we say has a positive or negative connotation.
- Hobbies help you rid your mind of recurring thoughts. Whether you are exercising, being artistic, playing music, or doing yoga, you consciously bring your attention to your body or your senses. By returning to whatever you

are doing, again and again, whenever your mind digresses, you practice mindfulness.
- Try not to use screens at least two hours before going to bed. The blue light signals your brain that it is still daylight and prevents the rise in melatonin (sleep hormone) that is necessary to fall asleep.
- End the day with gratitude. Remember five good things that happened that day.
- If possible, create five to ten minutes of quiet and calm before you go to sleep. Take a few breaths and centre yourself. Perhaps do a short body scan before falling asleep, gently concluding your day on a positive and connected note.

LIVING MINDFULLY CHECKLIST

✓ Keep bringing your awareness back to the current moment by connecting to the ground beneath the soles of your feet or to the chair on which you are sitting

✓ Intersperse your day with short meditations, focusing on the breath, using your breath as an anchor

✓ Single task instead of multitasking

✓ Slowdown in order to speed up

✓ See stress as a friend

✓ Be grateful and honour the good in your life, your family, friends, your work, your surroundings, and your home

✓ Accept what you cannot change

- ✓ Seed your day with small acts of kindness
- ✓ Be aware of the interaction between thoughts, feelings, body sensations, and behaviour
- ✓ Beware the wandering or monkey mind
- ✓ View difficult emotions as a messenger from your subconscious, befriend them, and allow them to rise and dissolve.
- ✓ Create a mindfulness reminder, like a gong on your smartphone, or an outside cue to make you pause and take a few breaths

*I have seen
A curious child, who dwelt upon a tract
Of inland ground, applying to his ear
The convolutions of a smooth-lipped shell
To which, in silence hushed, his very soul
Listened intensely; and his countenance soon
Brightened with joy; for from within were heard
Murmurings, whereby the monitor expressed
Mysterious union with it's native sea.
Even such a shell the universe itself
Is to the ear of Faith; and these are times,
I doubt not, when to you it doth impart
Authentic tidings of invisible things;
Of ebb and flow, and ever-during power;
And central peace, subsisting at the heart
of endless agitation.*

—**William Wordsworth, *The Excursion***

Part III
A Selection of Meditations

Chapter 15
For Grounding

*N*ow that you are motivated and well equipped to meditate, in this section I will talk about a few of my long-time favourite meditations. They come from different wisdom traditions and contemporary movements in mindfulness. I have grouped them so that you can choose a meditation for specific effects or intentions. Some of the meditations have a soundtrack that can be downloaded from my website.

ARRIVING IN THE PRESENT MOMENT

When: Use this meditation when starting your daily practice as it helps release tension in the body and mind and grounds one in the present moment

Meditation posture: Standing, sitting upright in a chair or on a cushion, or lying down

Duration: Five to fifteen minutes

Instructions:

1. Get in the meditation posture and make yourself comfortable. Become aware of the surface of the chair or cushion under your buttocks and the ground below you. Bring your attention to your feet if seated in a chair and feel the contact of the soles with the floor and the sensations that

are present in your feet right now. If seated on a meditation cushion, bring awareness to your legs and the area of the feet in contact with the ground. Now move your attention to your buttocks. Imagine having roots like a tree that grow deep down below the surface of the earth. In your mind's eye, you can visualise a connection that reaches to the centre of the earth. Feel a strong anchoring in the ground, giving you a feeling of stability and security. Allow yourself to be held by gravity.

2. Gently move your attention upwards. Attend to your upright spine—from the tailbone to the cervical spine in your neck, sensing each vertebra, until you reach your head. Become aware of your head and feel the connection to the space that surrounds the highest part of your body. Visualise your head as a small microcosm in the surrounding macrocosm. Connect to the space above the highest point of the head, the crown, and feel the connection upwards—to the universe, the sky or heaven, whatever resonates best with you.

3. Slowly bring your attention to the centre of your body, to your heart. Feel not only your physical heart but the entire energy field of the heart. Realise that this part of our body allows us to connect with other people. Become aware of the physical sensations that emanate from the heart. Feel the warmth and pleasant feeling of connection with yourself and radiating outwards. Allow your heart to open and expand.

4. Should you be meditating with others, imagine fine threads flowing from your hearts connecting you to one another as you sit together in a web of connection.

5. Before you conclude this meditation, become aware of your soles touching the ground and the contact of your buttocks and hip girdle with the cushion or surface of the chair you are sitting on. Visualise your entire body as it sits here, rooted to the ground through your lower body, and connected with the space above via the crown of your head. Sitting here in dignity, between heaven and earth, breathing and connected to your heart space.

6. Take three deep breaths at your own pace, feeling your entire body expand on the inbreath and gently relax on the outbreath. Inhaling and exhaling.

7. When you are ready, open your eyes and continue your day from this place of grounded strength. Be grateful for allowing yourself these moments of connecting to yourself.

THE UNIVERSE IN A RAISIN

Should you participate in an eight-week MBSR programme, the 'raisin' exercise will introduce you to the universe of mindfulness.

This activity of experiencing an 'unknown' object with all the five senses, along with observing the mind—as it interacts with the senses—allows one to come in contact with mindfulness experientially. It also introduces mindful eating. In the course of this exercise, a number of basic principles or attitudes can be observed, which correlate with one's behaviour in life. Whether it is the beginner's mind and the openness of a child, patience, presence, letting go of time-worn concepts and habits or acceptance, this meditation highlights various aspects of mindfulness.

The concept of the interconnection of all is introduced as we ponder on the lifecycle of a raisin, from a grape on a vine, ripening in the rays of the sun, it's harvest in rush baskets, often picked by hand and laid out to dry, so that the moisture evaporates, sorted and packed, and finally reaching the dining table in a cooked or baked dish. The raisin meditation makes us aware that everything is connected and is dependent on the other—nature, human beings, climate, business, technology, and the totality of individual and collective experience.

When: You want to experience mindful eating or mindfulness in practice

Meditation posture: Sitting in a chair

Duration: Ten to fifteen minutes

Instructions:

1. Prepare yourself for this exercise with a few raisins, a piece of chocolate, or any other dry fruit. In order to experience the spectrum of the senses and ingrained habits and opinions, try and embark upon this meditation with an open mind. Take the raisin to be an unknown object from outer space.

2. To begin with, take the unknown object and gently place it on your palm. Bring your full attention to it, imagining that you have never seen it before.

3. Observe the unknown object carefully, looking at it with full attention, letting your eyes explore it, taking in its shape, colour, and texture. Examine every feature of the object, whether it is shiny, or translucent, whether there are shadows, folds, ridges, hills, or valleys to be seen or whether it has any other unique visual aspects. The object may be dark or light, bright or dull, rough or smooth, solid or transparent. It may also have visible crystals or lines running within the gelatinous mass. Are there different shades of brown?

4. Move the object between your fingers and explore its texture. Apply light pressure to notice whether it is soft or hard. You might close your eyes if that helps you to focus and enhance your sense of touch. Recognising this is a raisin, note any thoughts you might have about raisins—any memories or associations about them or feelings of like or dislike. Sometimes recollections pop up of strudels or deserts, people associated (like grandmother, mother, favourite aunts, or friends), images of sun-soaked vineyards in the summer, and the perfume of ripening grapes in autumn.

5. Hold the object under your nose and inhale any aroma that arises. You may notice known or unknown smells. Become aware of any associations that may instinctively come to mind, like specific food, festivities, places, or family members. Bring awareness to any effect the smell may have in your mouth or stomach. Perhaps you may experience sudden salivation or experience hunger pangs.

6. Bring the object to your ear and gently tweak it between your thumb and index finger. Listen to the sounds it makes. Is there a soft squeaking or crackling as the sugar crystals burst? Even if it feels silly, just go along with the exercise, leaving cynicism aside.
7. Now bring the raisin slowly up to your mouth, noticing how your hand and arm know exactly how and where to position it and how your body gently moves its position. Becoming aware if you are salivating as the mind and body anticipate eating. Rub the raisin gently on your lower and upper lips and feel the texture. How different does it feel from the touch of your fingers?
8. Place the raisin gently in your mouth and let it remain there for a few seconds, exploring it with your tongue, feeling the sensations of having it there. Be aware of this pause and what it feels like to take some time before biting into the raisin. Does your anticipation grow, your stomach rumble?
9. Now take one or two conscious bites of the raisin and notice what happens, observing the taste and changing texture as you continue chewing and how it changes over time. Can you make out the sweetness, sourness, over-ripeness, saltiness, or experience waves of taste in the aftermath of the chewing? Has the form of the raisin changed in the process, it's surface? Remain awake, present, and curious with a beginner's mind.
10. When you are ready to swallow the raisin, experience the swallowing consciously and follow it as long as you can. Perhaps you can

detect the intention to swallow the raisin and when it arises.

11. Notice what remains of the raisin as you swallow and travels down your throat to your stomach. Is there a lingering taste in your mouth? How far down your throat can you feel the taste? Observe how you feel physically and emotionally after completing this exercise. Take a while to contemplate on this experience.

12. A lot of times during this exercise, participants instinctively connect to associations that bring about a realisation of the interconnectedness and interdependence of all things. For instance, 'the rays of the autumn sun falling on the grapes', 'the perfume of sweet grape juice', 'vineyards', 'summer picnics outdoors'. The images and feelings bring yet another dimension to the meditation, one which is personal and experiential.

Conclusion

What have you learnt from this exercise? Have you become aware of the role of your mind, existing opinions and judgements, cynicism, memories, past experiences, and associations? How did you react to the exercise in the first place and what changed in retrospect? Could you have a felt sense of the interconnectedness of all things?

The raisin meditation never fails to surprise, and the insights gleaned demonstrate the experience of mindfulness in daily living.

(Source: Adapted from the raisin exercise in the
MBSR programme)

THE THREE-MINUTE BREATHING SPACE

This is one of the basic practices of many mindfulness-based intervention programmes like MBSR or MBCT. The three-minute breathing space is a meditation that can be used whenever stress triggers, negative emotions, or disturbing thought patterns are observed. Originally developed for MBCT, this exercise has been adapted and introduced in many other settings.

This three-step process allows you to become aware of what is arising in the moment when you feel under pressure and it melts away negative patterns, often before you become aware of them. It is of great help in stressful situations. By pausing and breaking the circle, you ground yourself in the present moment and gain a greater sense of perspective, seeing things as they are in a larger dimension.

Sometimes depicted in the form of an hourglass, this three-step breathing space meditation has three distinct phases:

- Becoming aware
- Focusing and gathering attention to your breath
- Expanding attention

When: Any time you feel you need grounding; as often as you like

Meditation posture: Standing or seated in a chair

Duration: Three minutes

Instructions:

Step 1: Becoming aware

a) Adopt an erect and dignified posture, whether you are standing or sitting in a chair. You may close your eyes if you wish.

b) Then, bring your awareness to your inner experience and acknowledge it, asking: 'What is my experience right now?'
c) What thoughts are currently arising in your mind? Acknowledge your thoughts as mental events.
d) What body sensations are present in this moment? You may like to quickly scan your body to pick up any sensation of tightness or warmth or other phenomena. Acknowledge them, accept them as they come, and try not to change them.
e) What feelings are present here? Turn towards any sense of discomfort or unpleasantness without trying to make them different from how you find them.

Step 2: *Gathering and focusing attention on the breath*

a) Direct your attention to the physical sensations of the breath.
b) Feel the physical sensations of the breath in the abdomen . . . expanding as the breath moves into the body, and gently relaxing as the breath moves out.
c) Follow the breath all the way in and all the way out. Use each breath as an opportunity to anchor yourself into the present. And if your mind is distracted, gently bring your attention back to the breath.

Step 3: Expanding attention

a) Now, expand the field of awareness around the breathing pattern so that it includes a sense of the body, your posture, and facial expression as if the whole body was breathing. If you become aware of any sensations of discomfort or tension, you can bring the focus of your attention into the region and imagine that your breath can move into and around the area and sensations you are experiencing. By doing this you befriend them, without trying to change them in any way, accepting them as they are in this moment. Once they no longer hold your attention, return to the awareness of the whole body sitting here, moment by moment. Imagine the whole world is breathing with you.

The Hourglass Shape of the Breathing Space

The breathing space can be imagined in the shape of an hourglass. The wide opening at the top of an hourglass is similar to the first step of the breathing space. In this phase, you open your attention and gently acknowledge whatever is entering and leaving your awareness.

The second phase of the breathing space is like the narrowing of the hourglass's neck. It's where you focus your attention on the breath in the lower abdomen. You focus on the physical sensations of breathing, gently bringing the mind back to the breath when it wanders away or is distracted. This helps to anchor the mind—grounding you back into the present moment.

The third phase is the broad base of an hourglass where you open your awareness. Here, you are opening to life as it is, preparing yourself for the next moments of your day.

You reaffirm the sense that you have a place in the world, your whole mind-body, just as it is, in all its peace, dignity, and completeness.

(Source: Adapted from STOP, three-minute breathing space from the MBSR programme.)

That which sees through the eye but whom the eye sees not; that is the atman.
—***Mandukya Upanishad***

Chapter 16
FOR FOCUS AND CLARITY

BREATHING MEDITATION

Focusing on your breath is a basic mindfulness practice also called 'Shamatha' in Buddhism.

When: Use it as part of your daily routine as it will relax your body and improve focus and clarity

Meditation posture: Seated in a chair or on a cushion on the floor

Duration: Five to twenty minutes or longer

Instructions:

1. Take up a comfortable meditation posture with an upright spine, relaxed shoulders and arms, hands in your lap or placed on your thighs and your eyes closed or half-open, gently focused on the floor in front of you. Breathe through your nose.

2. When you have settled into the position, begin by bringing your attention to your breath as it moves gently in and out of the body. Should you feel any tension in your upper back, your shoulders, or lower back or elsewhere in your

body, breathe into this space and release the tension on the outbreath. Similarly, release any tension in your mind or emotions that are present as you exhale.
3. Observe the flow of breath and feel your body expand on the inhale and contract on the exhale. You can imagine a shaft of light entering your nostrils when you breathe in, feeling it move into the chest and raising the belly gently. And visualise the shaft of light as it leaves the body following it up from the abdomen, which slowly subsides through the chest and out of the nostrils when you breathe out. Maintain your focus on the breath, attending to the entire inbreath and the outbreath, allowing your breath to gently find its own rhythm.
4. If you feel comfortable, you can choose to count the breaths, starting at the end of every exhale—inhale and exhale, one; inhale and exhale, two—until you reach ten. Then counting backwards until you reach one again. Should you get lost, simply start counting from one again.
5. Sometimes it is helpful to choose an area in the body where you can feel the movement of the breath distinctly. This can be on the nostrils, the neck, the rise and fall of the chest, or the expansion and contraction of the belly. Choose the area that suits you best as a focus for experiencing the breathing body.
6. Feel your breath as it gently enters and leaves your body. With nothing to do, nowhere to go, and no control required. Just allow it to move naturally.

7. Feel the cool air enter your nostrils as you inhale and the warm breath on the exhale.
8. During the meditation it is possible that you get distracted. Images, feelings, sounds, emotions, or body sensations may arise. This is perfectly normal. If so, acknowledge whatever arises and keep bringing your attention back firmly and gently to observing your breath. This may happen ten times, twenty times, fifty times, or hundred times. Imagine your distractions as clouds in the sky, passing by in impermanence; not affecting the sky behind them. Accept things as they present themselves at this moment and constantly return to observing the breath as it moves in and out of the body. Moment by moment. Just the realisation that you have been distracted is an act of mindfulness.
9. Sit and focusing on the breath.
10. Now bring your attention back to your body. Become aware of your entire body and the connection to the floor beneath your feet or the seat of the chair. Feel your feet or knees on the ground and your buttocks on the cushion or chair. Take three deep breaths, attending to the areas in which you can feel your body expand and subside. Slowly open your eyes and take the pleasant feeling of stillness with you into the rest of your day.

If you practise regularly, you will find that your mind calms down. You will also be more present and focused in many areas of your life.

WALKING MEDITATION

A walking meditation is used in the same way as a breathing meditation to focus. We walk not to reach a destination but to experience the process of moving our feet and the contact with the earth or the ground below as we walk step by step. There is nothing that we must achieve except for mastering our attention in the present.

Walking meditations are practiced in many traditions. In Buddhist schools of meditation, walking meditations alternate with periods of sitting meditations. These are known as *kinhin* in the Zen Buddhist traditions of Japan, *Gyeongjaeng* in South Korea or *Kinh hành* in Vietnam. In Christianity, cloisters were an integral part of many monasteries, often in the form of a covered walk in the shape of a square or quadrangle. These were used for walking meditations and, even today, one can observe monks and nuns walking in silence. In India, a wandering or 'roaming about' meditation called *chankramanam* is practised, which is similar to the Buddhist walking meditation but incorporates the use of a mantra, either a personal one or the universal 'Om' at each step. Sufis, too, practice *Nazar bar Kadam* (Watch Your Step).

The concept of practising without effort can be challenging. This is because although our feet are physically walking, our mind is somewhere else. Our mind and body are seen as two separate entities and while our feet move in one direction, our attention pulls us into a different one. Our hectic lives, focused on getting somewhere or reaching a specific goal, do not permit us to walk for the sake of walking unless we are hiking or jogging. The simple act of walking can feel extraordinarily effortless and joyful once we realise the interdependence of our bodies and minds.

When we practice walking meditation, we arrive in each moment. Our regrets and sorrows gently fade away as we fully immerse ourselves in the present moment, and we discover all of life's wonders. As the great Vietnamese mindfulness master Thich Nhat Hanh wrote in *The Miracle of Mindfulness*, 'The mind can go in a thousand directions, but on this beautiful path, I walk in peace. With each step, the wind blows. With each step, a flower blooms.'

There are several different types of walking meditations that you can chose from depending on where you are or the duration you would like to walk for. Each type of walking meditation provides a different walking experience even though we have nowhere to go. Two walking meditations are introduced here. The first is based on a Buddhist meditation, often practiced in the Theravada schools, and the second is by Thich Nhat Hanh.

Theravada Walking Meditation

Choose a lane of about three to seven meters to carry out your walking meditation—by walking back and forth, pausing, and turning gently by 180 degrees when you reach each end of the lane. This meditation can be practiced barefoot in the garden, should the weather permit, and can be done anywhere else if you like, even in a small space.

Meditation posture: Walking—wherein your pace should be slow, regular, and even

Duration: Five to fifteen minutes

Instructions:

1. Stand upright, your feet hip-width apart. The soles of your feet must be in firm contact with

the ground. Attend to the connection of your feet with the floor below you.

2. Rock back and forth a few times to create a sense of stability. Are you leaning forward or backward? Are you balancing on the balls of your feet or on your heels? Ground yourself well before you start this walking practice and anchor your attention to the body.

3. Relax your shoulders and facial muscles. Your chin should slightly tilt downwards. Your hands should lie loosely folded on one another—with the palms facing inwards. You can also rest your hands slightly under your navel or place them on your lower back by holding one wrist gently with the other hand. Keep your eyes open and focus on a spot on the ground about one meter ahead of you. Do not forget to smile because it releases happy hormones in the body.

4. You may scan your body before beginning the meditation. Start at your feet and notice the sensations, thoughts, and emotions present. Try and release them by exhaling deeply. Visualise them flowing onto the floor below you. Now you are ready to begin your meditation.

5. Slowly and attentively raise the foot of your left leg. Consciously notice your thigh and calf muscles tightening and how your body tilts slightly forward to maintain its balance. As you raise your foot, observe it as it moves upwards in a semicircle and attend to your foot as you place it on the floor. Keep your foot on the ground, with your heel first, and then gently bring the sole and the toes in contact with the floor.

6. As you carefully place the left foot on the ground, lift the heel of the right foot off the floor. Observe the right foot lift off the ground, suspend it in the air, slowly lower it, and place it in front of the left foot. Continue walking in this fashion with ease. Raising, suspending, lowering, connecting. Step by step. Moment by moment.

7. You may also coordinate your breath with each step—breathing in when you raise and lower your left foot and breathing out when you raise and lower your right foot. Or breathing in and out at your own rhythm.

8. You may, if you like, synchronise your steps with a meditation of loving-kindness by saying the following to yourself: 'May I be happy. May I be healthy and free from suffering. May I be at peace' or 'May all beings be happy. May all beings be healthy and free from suffering. May they be at peace.'

9. Perhaps you become aware that your mind is being distracted by thoughts, images, body sensations, emotions, or stories. Take note of whatever is occurring and bring your attention firmly back to feeling the ground below you.

10. Just keep going at your own pace, perceiving the flow of the movement. Raising, suspending, lowering, connecting. Step by step. Moment by moment. A harmonious sequence of steps.

11. When you reach the end of the lane, rest for a moment or two, acknowledge your surroundings, and turn 180 degrees to continue your walking experience. Walk back and forth and take in the movement of your foot on each step.

12. After the chosen period is over, end your walking meditation. Shake your legs and thank yourself for taking this time off for yourself.

You may feel a bit shaky or out of balance when you begin. This is normal and will improve after some practise. Should you have difficulty maintaining your balance, you can walk along a wall so that you can support yourself with your hand. You can also try out different walking tempos—walking slowly, extremely slowly—and carefully observing.

Thich Nhat Hanh Walking Meditation

Often called the father of western mindfulness, the exceptional master and peace activist, the late Thich Nhat Hanh, propagated affirmations to produce positive mental states whilst walking.

Meditation posture: Walking slowly and gently

Duration: Ten to fifteen minutes

Instructions:

1. Walk gently and slowly and be aware of each movement, of each step as you walk. Focus on the present moment by connecting to your body, the soles of your feet, and your breath.
2. Repeat one of the following affirmations as you take a step, feeling a deep sense of gratitude and love:
   - Breathing in, say, 'I have arrived'; breathing out, say, 'I am home'
   - Breathing in, say, 'In the here'; breathing out, say, 'In the now'

- Breathing in, say, 'I am solid'; breathing out, say, 'I am free'
- Breathing in, say, 'In the ultimate'; breathing out, say, 'I dwell'

This meditation will be a wonderful experience if you walk barefoot in the grass, fully aware of the ground under your feet. Feeling the softness of the grass, moisture, the solid ground, the cool air, the tickling of the grass, sinking into the moss, and the dry leaves or small twigs and pebbles make the liveness of the earth palpable as you walk.

LISTENING MEDITATION

A listening meditation uses sound as an anchor. We are surrounded by a universe of sound in the form of noise, vibration, hum, or echoes emanating from outside our bodies or from within. To enhance the transfer of formal meditation to our lives, it can be helpful to open oneself to the sounds arising in the present moment. Listening without judging to sounds that are here now. A sound only occurs in the present moment, and they cannot be experienced in the past or the future, making us ground ourselves in the here and now.

Instead of using the breath as an object of meditation, it sometimes can be helpful—especially for people who have difficulty breathing—to follow a listening meditation by focusing on sounds that arise both externally and internally. This meditation is equally useful if you are suffering from asthma or other breathing disorders. Occasionally, the breath can evoke a feeling of suffocation.

A listening meditation can be done in different ways. You can either listen to and accept all that is arising in the space of sound, or you can practice by listening to a piece of music with attention and awareness.

a) Listen to and accepting the sound space arising in the current moment without interpreting, labelling, liking, or disliking what arises, or searching for the source. Allow the sound to come to your ears, do not look for it. Become the hearing, sound by sound.

b) Listen to a piece of music with attention and awareness. Take in the instruments playing, the pitch, the tone, the atmosphere being created, the rhythm, the speed, and all the other aspects that the music evokes in you. Just accepting it as it is.

When: For focus and to ground yourself in the current moment

Meditation posture: Sitting or lying down

Duration: Ten to twenty minutes

Instructions:

1. Take a comfortable seat with an upright spine, relaxing your body, with your feet firmly placed on the ground. This allows a feeling of stability and security. You can also close your eyes or let your eyes focus on the floor in front of you. Become aware of what your mind is currently dwelling on, accepting it for what it is. In case you prefer to lie down, find a comfortable position on a mat or in your bed and cover yourself with a light blanket. Feel the gravity pulling you into a safe and protected space.

2. Gently bring your attention to your breath. Feel each inbreath as it moves into the body, causing the abdomen and chest to rise, and feel each

outbreath as it leaves the body, resulting in a falling of the abdomen and chest. Become aware of the movement of the breath in the front, in the back, on either side and inside your body feeling any sensations that arise.

3. Observe the rhythm and quality of the breath as it moves gently in and out of the body, just by itself. Without any force or manipulation. Allow the breath to settle into its natural rhythm.

4. Now let your breath recede from your focus and bring your attention to your hearing. Let your awareness rest on the natural perception of listening and on the sounds and noises in your surroundings. If you become aware of sounds, then just listen . . . let the sounds reach you, do not search for them. How does this feel? Just sitting and listening . . . What can you hear now?

5. Where is the sound coming from? Is it here in this room? You may observe that some sounds appear as if they are close by, others from further away, and some reach you from a far away. Is the sound coming from your body? A gurgling, rumbling, snorting, gasping, or a joint popping sound? Register whatever is reaching you at this moment with acceptance.

6. Observe the sounds arising like a neutral observer, without labelling them as known or unknown, good or disturbing, liking or disliking, wanting more or rejecting. Just listen, moment by moment. Maybe you can explore the space between the sounds or become aware of the stillness. Become the awareness itself. Let the sounds come to you.

7. You can imagine your body is like an antenna, receiving all sound vibrations, unconcerned with the source, intensity, timbre, or decibel and is receptive to all that is reaching your eardrums. Here. Now. At this very moment.
8. Where is your mind now? Have distractions pulled your attention away from your focus on the soundscape? If so, bring your attention firmly back to observing your current world of sound and noise, letting each distraction be registered and letting them go, moment by moment. Use the soundscape as an anchor in the present moment.
9. Sit with an open mind and awareness for sound as sometimes the sound waves stay for a while, repeating themselves, or some are extremely short, some long. But ultimately, they all dissolve like clouds. Be one with sensing the hearing from moment to moment. Sounds appear and disappear in the vast space of awareness.
10. Now gently allow the sounds to disappear into the background and bring your attention back to your breath.
11. Stay with the breath for a while. Just observing, watching, feeling the in- and outbreath, and the universe that opens by just being with the breath.
12. Before bringing the meditation to a close, take three deep breaths, feeling your body moving gently.
13. Open your eyes.

The morning sea of silence broke into ripples of bird songs;
and the flowers were all merry by the roadside;
and the wealth of gold was scattered through the rift of the clouds
while we busily went on our way and paid no heed.
    We sang no glad songs nor played;
    we went not to the village for barter;
    we spoke not a word nor smiled;
    we lingered not on the way.
We quickened our pace more and more as the time sped by.
The sun rose to the mid sky and doves cooed in the shade.
Withered leaves danced and whirled in the hot air of noon.
The shepherd boy drowsed and dreamed in the shadow of
    the banyan tree,
    and I laid myself down by the water
    and stretched my tired limbs on the grass.
    My companions laughed at me in scorn;
    they held their heads high and hurried on;
    they never looked back nor rested;
    they vanished in the distant blue haze.
    They crossed many meadows and hills,
    and passed through strange, far-away countries.
All honour to you, heroic host of the interminable path!
    Mockery and reproach pricked me to rise,
    but found no response in me.
    I gave myself up for lost
in the depth of a glad humiliation-in the shadow of a dim
    delight.

... contd.

*The repose of the sun-embroidered green gloom
slowly spread over my heart.
I forgot for what I had travelled,
and I surrendered my mind without struggle
to the maze of shadows and songs.
At last, when I woke from my slumber and opened my
eyes,
I saw thee standing by me, flooding my sleep with thy
smile.
How I had feared that the path was long and wearisome,
and the struggle to reach thee was hard!*
—The Journey by Rabindranath Tagore

Chapter 17
For Resilience

BODY-SCAN MEDITATION

When: You feel the need for relaxation

Meditation posture: Seated or (preferably) lying down

Duration: Ten to forty minutes

Instructions:

1. Take a comfortable position in a chair and sit straight, your body should be in the meditation posture. In case you prefer to lie down, stretch yourself out on your back with legs straight and feet slightly apart, and place your arms alongside your torso. Close your eyes and breathe gently through the nose. Feel the connection to the floor below you and with every outbreath become aware of your body sinking deeper and deeper into the mat. The ground and the force of gravity are supporting and carrying you just like the seat of the chair and your feet, giving you a sense of security and comfort.

2. During this meditation, you will be taking a journey through your body, in which you will sense into the different parts of your body. What sensations can you feel arising? Where is your mind? Begin from the toes of your left foot and

gently travel upwards to your crown. Just as with the other meditations, should you get distracted, bring your attention gently and firmly back to connecting to the sensations in the body.

3. When you are ready, bring your attention to your feet. Start by becoming aware of your toes. Is it possible to feel each toe individually? What sensations are currently arising in your toes and feet? Can you experience warmth or coolness? Or are there sensations of throbbing, pain, or tingling present? Possibly you can feel nothing at all, which is okay. Accept whatever shows itself. Gently move towards the soles of your feet, the back of your feet, to your heels, and become aware of sensations present in your feet. Does your left foot feel different from your right foot?

4. Now slowly move your attention upwards. From your feet move towards your ankles, calves, knees, and thighs, and finally to your hip joints. What is arising in each region of your legs? Accept every sensation or no sensation as it is, without wanting to change anything, without judging whether good or bad or labelling anything.

5. Move your attention from your legs to your spine. Travel up your spinal cord, vertebra by vertebra, from the tailbone to your sacrum, then to the lumbar and thoracic spine, finally arriving at the cervical spine in the upper body. Become aware of your shoulder girdle and the shoulder blades. What is arising in the backbone at this moment?

6. Gently allow your spine to fade from your focus, and bring your attention to your lower abdomen, upper abdomen, chest, and all the organs situated in these parts of the body. Attend fully to your organs. What sensations are arising here? Now, let this region fade into the background.
7. Finally bring your attention to both your arms, flowing down from your shoulders to your fingertips. Become aware of each finger, the front and back of your hands, and your wrists. Feel what is showing itself in the present moment. Then move towards to your lower arms, elbows, upper arms, the shoulders, the neck, and the head. What sensations are present here?
8. Feel the contact of the skin with the fabric of your clothes. Maybe you can experience the air caressing your skin? In case your thoughts have wound themselves up in infinite circles, let them go and bring your attention back to connecting with the body.
9. Attend to your face, your eyes, your ears, your nose, and forehead . . . to the tiny muscles in your face. Feel the highest point on the body, the crown of your head.
10. Now become aware of your entire body as it sits or lies here in proprioception. What does it feel like? Warm? Alive? Breathing? Enjoy the deep connection with your body.
11. Bring your awareness to your breath and feel the breathing space of your body expand when you inhale and relax when you exhale. Take a few breaths, simply staying with your breathing.

12. Bring the body scan to a close by becoming aware of the contact to the floor or the seat of the chair. Move your toes and fingers. Gently stretch your body by raising your arms above your head. Become aware of your surroundings and when you feel ready, open your eyes and return to your activities of the day, taking with you a feeling of relaxation and body awareness.

(*Source*: Adapted from the body scan of the MBSR programme)

STANDING MINDFUL MOVEMENTS

When: After several hours of sitting and no movement

Meditation posture: Standing

Duration: Ten to twenty minutes

Instructions:

1. Stand straight with your feet hip-width apart and parallel to each other. Your spine must be upright, core somewhat tight so that you are in a stable and grounded posture, your arms should hang loosely on the side, and relax your shoulders. The neck and head should be straight and in balance, and your eyes should be open during this exercise. Breath through the nose. Gently bring your attention to your feet. Become aware of the surface on which you are standing. Is it hard or soft? Smooth or rough? Even or uneven? Ground yourself and stand like a mountain, anchored and secure.

2. Now lean forward with the entire length of your body and observe how far you can go comfortably. Stay in this position for a few

breaths and then move back to the starting position. Now lean backwards and see how far you can manage to do so. Stay in this position for a few moments before bringing yourself back to the starting position. Take a few deep breaths and notice what your body is experiencing.

3. Now tilt your body to the left. Keep your feet firmly anchored to the ground. Breathe in and out a few times in this position, and then return your body to its original position. Now tilt your entire body to the right. Take a few breaths and return to the original position. Become aware of what the body feels like after these movements.

4. Take a short break.

5. With the next inhalation, lift your arms horizontally to the right and left at the same time and bring them towards the ceiling, palms facing inwards. Stretch upwards. If you like, you can raise your heels off the floor and stand on your toes, feeling the stretch in the entire body. Then interlock your fingers and stretch the arms upwards as much you can. Feel the stretch in your arms, armpits, chest, back, legs. Let your breath flow freely as you stretch, bringing awareness to the entire body.

6. Release your fingers and lower the arms again with an exhalation until they hang loosely on either side of your body. Repeat this exercise a second time.

7. After you have finished, bring your attention to feel the sensations that this stretching exercise has left in the body. Take three conscious deep breaths and close the mindful movement exercise.

DEALING WITH EMOTIONS

When: Whenever difficult emotions like anger, fear, anxiety, or the feeling of overwhelm arise, this short meditation helps one return to their inner balance

Meditation posture: Seated

Duration: Five to ten minutes

Instructions:

1. Find a place where you can be undisturbed for some time. Take a comfortable meditation posture with an upright spine and your feet firmly placed on the floor. You may close your eyes or keep them half-open and slightly lowered. Breathe through your nostrils.
2. Bring your attention to your breathing. Feel your breath moving in and out of your body effortlessly. Follow the inhalation and exhalation for approximately twenty breaths.
3. Now become aware of your body as a whole—your chest, your abdomen, your skin, and your current emotional state.
4. Observe the emotions or feelings that arise in the moment. This can range from anger, boredom, resentment, fear, or worry. Try and look at it lightly, without deliberately displacing or negating it. Keep your attention on the emotion(s).
5. Observe and feel what your body is expressing in the moment. Carefully scan your body from the soles of your feet up to the crown of your head. What is currently arising? Just be with what the

body is experiencing. Are there sensations of burning, tightness, lightness, pressure, warmth, expansion, throbbing, or anything else? Accept these sensations as they are in the present moment. Where do you feel a sensation in the body? Can you link it to the emotion you are experiencing?

6. Connect the body sensation with the emotion. Label it—calling it anger, love, sadness, etc. You will find that emotions evoke consistent reactions in the body. Whenever you experience an emotion, bring yourself to feel the body sensation associated with it.

7. Release ideas and self-talk about the causes of the arising emotion. The storytelling mind, images, memories, or other thoughts may distract you. Let these pass by. Just focus on remaining with the difficult emotion. Perhaps you will observe that the emotion will gently dissolve on its own. Feel the stillness set in.

8. Watch your feelings again. Are you the same as before or different? What has changed?

9. End the meditation by coming back to your breath. Bring your attention to the body and the contact of the feet with the floor. Become aware of your surroundings.

10. Open your eyes and bring this meditation to a close.

A human being is a part of the whole called by us universe, a part limited in time and space. He experiences himself, his thoughts and feeling as something separated from the rest, a kind of optical delusion of his consciousness. This delusion is a kind of prison for us, restricting us to our personal desires and to affection for a few persons nearest to us. Our task must be to free ourselves from this prison by widening our circle of compassion to embrace all living creatures and the whole of nature in its beauty.
—**Albert Einstein**

Chapter 18

For an Open Heart

*D*istress, emotional overwhelm, impermanence, worry about the future, fear, cruelty, sorrow, dealing with the unknown are some of the factors we face, especially in the times of disruption. Each human being experiences elements of emotional disconnect, sometimes resulting in deep-seated trauma or requiring psychological help. Allowing ourselves to open towards our own misery or discomfort and to the woes of others shows that all kinds of suffering is universal. It is not confined to age, sex, origin, or education but is a part of the human journey.

To feel the connection between us as humans it sometimes helps to pose a few questions that are common to humankind. In asking ourselves, 'Do I want to suffer?', 'Do others want to suffer?', 'Do I want others—including people I dislike—to suffer?' we address an elemental aspect of collective living.

In everything that we think, say, or do, we consider these few attitudes before we act like: 'Does this thought/speech/action bring suffering to me?' or 'Does this thought/speech/action bring suffering to others?' or 'Does this thought/speech/action relieve my suffering?' or 'Does this thought/speech/action relieve others' suffering?' Just answering these simple questions supports a more empathetic and compassionate way of meeting others. And when we see ourselves as mirrors, it is about seeing ourselves in others . . . of accepting ourselves and others just as we are and the commonality of being human.

LOVING-KINDNESS FOR YOURSELF AND OTHERS

When: In times of disruption and distress

Meditation posture: Seated

Duration: Five to twenty minutes

Instructions:

1. Take a comfortable seat, keeping your back upright, and connect to the ground below you with the soles of your feet. Start by focusing your attention on your breath and ride on the waves of inhalation and exhalation for a few breaths. Arrive and ground yourself before you begin with this meditatio

2. Now bring your attention to the area of your heart. How does it feel? If you like, you can put a hand, or both hands—cupping the left palm in the right—on your heart. Keep it there during the practice if it feels right. Try and envision love and kindness emanating from the centre of your chest and filling your body with warmth and compassion. If you like, you can imagine beams of light emerging from the centre of your chest.

3. In loving-kindness meditation, we repeat several good wishes for the benefit of ourselves, our loved ones, a neutral person who we don't know well, a person with whom we have difficulties, and for all sentient beings on this planet. These wishes can be as follows or you can formulate them as you like:

    i. May all beings be happy and content or I wish . . .
    ii. May all beings be healthy and free from disease and pain or I wish . . .
    iii. May all beings live in peace and security, or I wish . . .
    iv. May all beings be free from fear and walk through life with serenity or I wish . . .
    v. May all beings be at peace and live with lightness of being . . .

4. Beginning with ourselves, we send ourselves good wishes like: 'May I be happy and content. May I be healthy and free from disease and pain. May I find peace and security.'

5. Now turn to people you love. Let these people appear before your inner eye and wish them well. Extend loving compassion to your family and friends and let yourself be touched inwardly whilst you do so. Formulate positive wishes for your loved ones: 'May you be happy and content. May you be healthy and free from disease and pain. May you find peace and security.' Linger a little thereafter. Good wishes can be repeated several times. Let them touch your heart when you repeat them.

6. Now send these good wishes to neutral individuals like the postman, a shopkeeper, or bus conductor.

7. Then bring your attention and good wishes to a person with whom you have not had good relations. If you're a beginner of this meditation, try not to choose a person who has inflicted much

pain on you. But keep the difficulty between you simple: 'May you be happy and content. May you be healthy and free from disease and pain. May you find peace and security.'

8. Finally, let your compassion expand and embrace the planet with all its sentient beings. People living North and South, East and West, in war-torn zones, in regions of drought, in areas of disaster, in hospitals and refugee camps, in places of suffering and pandemic. If you like, you can also include animals, fish, insects, and plants. Sending all sentient beings wishes of goodwill: 'May you be happy and content. May you be healthy and free from pain and disease. May you find peace and security.'

9. In expressing loving-kindness, let it arise from your heart and do not make it just a mental exercise. The power of this meditation lies in expressing these wishes with an intrinsic desire to help others.

10. Finish this exercise by consciously letting the images of sentient beings recede from your mind and by bringing your attention back to your breath for a few minutes. Observe it gently move in and out of your body . . . breath by breath, moment by moment. Then open your eyes and conclude the meditation. Perhaps you can feel a difference in your chest, where your heart lies. You might also discover a tinge of joy, tingling or warmth in your heart.

SELF-COMPASSION: TOUCHING YOUR HEART MEDITATION

This exercise allows you to gently sooth and touch yourself whenever we are not feeling good. It is often helpful to put a hand on your heart and feel the warmth emanating from the middle of your chest or to hug yourself lovingly with both arms. It may seem slightly strange at first, but your body can feel the contact and reacts to the attention given.

The body reacts to physical contact and affection in the same way a baby or child reacts to their mother's embrace. Research shows that physical touch leads to the release of the 'cuddle' or 'love' hormone oxytocin that is produced in larger quantities after birth and has a calming effect. Oxytocin is part of our emotion regulation systems and is responsible for the feeling of security in the body. In that we give and receive care and kindness ourselves, our limbic system returns to harmony.

When: Any time of day you are not feeling good

Meditation posture: Seated

Duration: Ten minutes

Instructions:

1. Sit upright on a chair or on a cushion. Relax your body.
2. Consciously breathe in and out deeply two to three times and connect with the flow of your breath. Feel the gentle inhale and exhale on the tip of your nose and slowly find the rhythm of your breath.
3. Gently place a hand onto your heart and feel its gentle pressure and warmth. You can also

put both your hands on your chest and feel the different sensations. Become aware of the contact between the skin of both the hands and the region of your chest. You can make small, circular movements with your fingers.

4. Feel the natural movement of the body, the expansion and relaxation during inhalation and exhalation. Remain with this self-compassion meditation for as long as you want.
5. Bring a smile to your lips and breathe gently into your heart. Invite it to open and expand.
6. While you are breathing gently, in complete connection with your hands on your chest, perceive what is happening inside your body. Is it possible to receive this comforting touch? Do you notice any effects on your mood? Accept everything as it is in this moment.
7. When you would like to conclude this meditation, become aware of the soft and regular constant flow of your breath. Stay with your breath for a few moments.
8. Bring your attention gently back to the outer world. When you feel ready, open your eyes and conclude this meditation.

Some people are uncomfortable with keeping their hands on their hearts. If it is the case with you, try out where you think a gentle touch feels soothing. You can try one of the following gestures:

i. Place a hand on your cheek
ii. Cup your face with both hands
iii. Gently stroke your arm

iv. Fold your arms over one another in front of your chest and hug yourself gently
v. Make small, circular, or caressing movements on your chest
vi. Place a hand on your abdomen
vii. Place one hand on your abdomen and one hand on your chest
viii. Fold your hands in your lap

Perhaps it is possible to make this short meditation a habit whenever you feel you need a bit of self-compassion. You will learn to sense clearly whether your heart feels warm or cold, wide or narrow, open or close, light or heavy, and what it needs to feel secure and loved in the moment. Sometimes a gentle caress of the heart space with your hand, a friendly word, word of comfort, or a calming rhythm of the breath can evoke this feeling.

By performing this heart exercise whenever required, you remember how easy it can be to treat yourself lovingly and with compassion.

*The Bodhisattva of Compassion,
When he meditated deeply,
Saw the emptiness of all five skandhas
And sundered the bonds that caused him suffering.
Here then,
Form is no other than emptiness,
Emptiness no other than form.
Form is only emptiness,
Emptiness only form.
Feeling, thought, and choice,
Consciousness itself,
Are the same as this.
All things are by nature void
They are not born or destroyed
Nor are they stained or pure
Nor do they wax or wane
So, in emptiness, no form,
No feeling, thought, or choice,
Nor is there consciousness.
No eye, ear, nose, tongue, body, mind;
No colour, sound, smell, taste, touch,
Or what the mind takes hold of,
Nor even act of sensing.
No ignorance or end of it,
Nor all that comes of ignorance;
No withering, no death,
No end of them.
Nor is there pain, or cause of pain,
Or cease in pain, or noble path
To lead from pain;
Not even wisdom to attain!
Attainment too is emptiness.
So know that the Bodhisattva*

*Holding to nothing whatever,
But dwelling in Prajna wisdom,
Is freed of delusive hindrance,
Rid of the fear bred by it,
And reaches clearest Nirvana.
All Buddhas of past and present,
Buddhas of future time,
Using this Prajna wisdom,
Come to full and perfect vision.
Hear then the great dharani,
The radiant peerless mantra,
The Prajnaparamita
Whose words allay all pain;
Hear and believe its truth!*

*Gate Gate Paragate Parasamgate
Bodhi Svaha
Gate Gate Paragate Parasamgate
Bodhi Svaha
Gate Gate Paragate Parasamgate
Bodhi Svaha*
—The Heart Sutra as recited in the Triratna Buddhist Community

Chapter 19
For Giving and Taking

Tonglen Meditation

'Tonglen' in Tibetan stands for giving (*tong*) and taking (*len*). This meditation is highly effective in transforming one's self-centred attitude into appreciation for others. The giving and taking meditation exchanges attachment and rejection with loving-kindness and compassion.

This meditation uses the breath as an anchor for visualisation. Breath in to take in all the suffering and wish: 'May I take on all the suffering of this being however much it may be.' Breath out to wish: 'May all my love and compassion reach every sentient being. May you be free from suffering and the causes of suffering. May you be well and happy.'

Imagine your mental suffering in the form of a black cloud that fills your body. With each inhalation, visualise pulling this dark cloud into a bright light in the middle of your chest, next to your heart, to completely dissolve it there. With each exhalation, you breathe out compassion, thus dissolving any sadness and suffering that you may have breathed into your heart. Sometimes this exercise can invoke feelings of suffocation. An alternative is to imagine that you are taking the sorrow away and exchanging it for good wishes, kindness, and compassion.

When: In others' difficult situations or before a meeting with a stranger

Meditation posture: Seated

Duration: Five to ten minutes

Instructions:

1. Start by using Tonglen to cultivate kindness and compassion for yourself.
2. Let the thought rise: 'May I be free of suffering and its causes. May I be happy and healthy.'
3. Inhale with compassion, release, and extinguish the suffering in your heart. Exhale loving-kindness and send yourself everything you need to feel happiness and contentment. Repeat these wishes of taking and giving a few times slowly and softly. Then let yourself fade into the background.
4. Now expand the field of loving-kindness and compassion to near ones, friends, or family members who may be experiencing any form of suffering—someone who is unwell, is grieving, has lost a partner, parent, family member, or friend, or to someone who lost their job or other sufferings. And say: 'May you be free of suffering and its causes. May you be happy and healthy.'
5. Breathing with compassion on the inbreath. Breathing with loving-kindness on the outbreath. Feel the suffering move into your heart space and the rays of light and goodness move out of every pore of your body. Focus on this person for a few breaths.

6. Gently let the person recede into the background.
7. Next, expand the field of compassion to strangers or those with whom you have difficulties and wish them well with all your heart: 'May you be free from suffering and its causes. May you be healthy and happy.'
8. Inhale with compassion. Exhale with loving-kindness. Similarly experiencing your connection to the suffering of the others and the loving-kindness.
9. If you like you can extend the field to all sentient beings on our planet, drawing in their suffering of hunger, pain, disease, war, poverty, delusion, and illness, and send out loving-kindness from the centre of your heart: 'May you be free from suffering and the causes of suffering. May you be healthy and happy.'
10. Repeat these wishes a few times as you breathe in their suffering, with compassion, and breathe out loving-kindness. Breath by breath . . . fully present, fully aware.
11. Gently let these beings withdraw from your field of compassion. Bring your awareness to your heart and feel any sensations that arise in your body. When you feel ready, bring the meditation to a close.

JUST LIKE ME MEDITATION

This exercise can be performed alone and/or in groups of two people. If you are a larger group, then split into pairs, move your chair (or cushion) to face the person opposite you. Briefly exchange names in case you do not know each other. Keep this seating position for the entire meditation.

In case you are alone, bring to your mind a person who means a lot to you for this meditation. Visualise this person in front of your mind's eye.

When: To feel connected—for friendships, kindness, and affection

Meditation posture: Seated

Duration: Ten to twenty minutes

Instructions:

1. Sit in comfortable meditation posture with an upright spine and your feet placed firmly on the ground, aware of the contact to the ground. Your shoulders and arms are relaxed, and your eyes are closed, to begin with. Should this be uncomfortable for you, then keep your eyes partially open with your gaze averted. Breathe through the nose.

2. Bring your attention to your breath for a few moments as you gently arrive fully in your body. Be present, awake, and connected to the intention of the exercise. Repeat or read the following sentences in silence:

> Just like me,
> This person in front of me has a body and mind, just like me.
> This person in front of me has emotions, feelings, and thoughts, just like me.

This person in front of me has been sad, disappointed, angry, hurt, or confused sometimes in their life, just like me.

This person in front of me has experienced pain and suffering, just like me.

This person seated in front of me also wants to be free from pain and suffering, just like me.

This person seated in front of me wants to be healthy, to be loved, and to have fulfilling relationships, just like me.

This person wants to be happy, just like me.

Just like me.

Let these thoughts fill your being as you voice these sentiments.

3. Now let positive wishes for this person arise in you. You may like to use the following sentences or anything else you feel more comfortable with: 'May you have the strength and support to overcome any difficulties that life might have in store for you. May you be free of pain and suffering. May you be happy because you are a fellow human being just like me.'
4. Now take a moment to look at your partner. Then close your eyes again or, if you prefer, lower your gaze.
5. If you wish you may extend wishes for happiness and well-being to everyone in the room: 'May everyone be happy. May they be well.'

6. You may also extend this wish for well-being even further to all those you know and to all the beings on this planet: 'May you be happy. May you be well.'
7. Now gently open your eyes, stretch if needed, and return your awareness to the room.

    You now have a few minutes to talk to your partner about how the experience was for each of you.

(*Source*: Adapted from programmes that develop emotional intelligence)

*To see a World in a Grain of Sand
And a Heaven in a Wild Flower
Hold Infinity in the palm of your hand
And Eternity in an hour.*
—*Auguries of Innocence,* **William Blake**

Chapter 20
For Creativity and Innovative Thinking

Journalling

Journalling is a proven method of allowing the subconscious to emerge. Like keeping a diary, it encourages you to write down your thoughts and feelings without adhering to a particular structure.

Writing is a process that promotes creativity. Both the hemispheres of the brain are activated, with the writing activity controlled by the left hemisphere of the brain and creativity by the right.

To start, you will need a notebook or a few sheets of paper and a pen. Look for a place where you are undisturbed. Set a timer or alarm to remind you in case you decide on a specific time for the exercise. The suggested time is twenty minutes.

Before you start, consciously take a few deep breaths to focus your attention inward. Be open to everything that wants to show itself. When you feel you have arrived in your body, start writing. Continue writing down whatever comes to mind without pausing—be it feelings, descriptions, fragments of poetry, thoughts, plans, doodles, or drawings.

Simple Mindful Journalling Techniques to Get Started

- Write in detail about your day, recording your emotions, thoughts, and reactions to events that happened. It is often a nice way to summarise and end your day, a bit like a mindful diary. What would you like to remember? What was unexpected? Did you have any encounters?
- A gratitude journal is a wonderful method to bring more gratitude into your life. Recall a few things every day for which you are grateful and write them down. The positivity created by gratitude cultivates the formation of 'gratitude neurons', memories that you can fall back on when you are feeling low.

Sometimes it is helpful to trigger the flow of writing with a question. Questions can range from: 'What was I pleased about today?' or 'What am I grateful for?' Journalling unlocks new insights and helps one know themselves better. Goals and unclear ideas, too, are often resolved by writing.

OPEN AWARENESS

When: For creativity and beginner's mind

Meditation posture: Seated

Duration: Ten to twenty minutes

Instructions:

1. Take your meditation posture with an upright back and a comfortable sitting position. Relax.
2. Take a few breaths and watch your breath flow in and out of your body.

3. Observe your breath for a few minutes before you begin this practice. Use your breath as an anchor and keep coming back to it should you feel overwhelmed during this meditation.
4. Release your focus from the breath and allow your consciousness to open as if you were expanding. Like a fan or umbrella or a blooming flower, let your awareness spread wide.
5. Observe what is occurring moment by moment. Watch sounds, thoughts, body sensations, emotions, images, or other experiences arising from within. Watch how everything arises, lingers for a while, and then fades. Perceive with wakeful interest and curiosity what is emerging without becoming entangled in judgment, attachment, rejection, like, or dislike. Leave aside the storytelling mind firmly and gently. Just watch the screen of open awareness with detachment and interest.
6. If you like, consider the fact that everything is impermanent, changing from moment to moment. How about you, the observer? Are you permanent, or could you be changing from moment to moment, too? If there is no fixed, stable, and solid self, is it possible to change ourselves, our attitude, our perspective, and ways of being? Allowing new possibilities to arise?
7. Should you get lost in the space of open awareness, bring your attention back to the anchor of your breath for a few moments. When you feel comfortable and secure, expand your consciousness once again and continue observing your experiences.

8. After a few minutes, take a few deep, conscious breaths and bring back your attention to your surroundings. Feel the ground below you and the connection of your body with the cushion or chair you are seated upon. Gently open your eyes and bring the meditation to a close.

Try and take this feeling of open awareness with you into the rest of your day. Just as we encounter sensations, thoughts, and other experiences during our meditation, our life provides us with a constant stream of distractions in various forms. Learn to take a step back and view them with equanimity.

BREAK MEDITATION

Just taking a break for a few minutes from what you are doing gives your body and mind an immense energy surge. Most of us work incessantly at a task or activity, be it in an organisation or as an independent professional. Breaks are usually taken at lunch but rarely in between. Recent research has shown that employees who took regular breaks had less emotional exhaustion, less stress, demonstrated more creativity, better overall well-being, and higher job satisfaction. The study also revealed that the timing and quality of breaks were significant. Employee performance and well-being benefitted most from breaks that were unrelated to work, for instance, a coffee break, a short walk, a mindfulness exercise, or social interaction, and were taken early and more frequently in the day.

Taking a break shifts your brain from a conceptual mode to an experiential mode and moves you from doing to being. Below are a few tips for break time activities:

- Look out of the window for a few minutes, taking in what surrounds you outside
- Stop and look at the sky, watch the clouds or the sunrays
- Stand up and move your body mindfully—stretch, bend your body sideways, backwards, and to the front
- Turn your face away from the screen by looking left or right for a few breaths
- Walk a few steps back and forth next to your desk

When: To recharge your mind and brain

Meditation posture: Seated or standing

Duration: For three breaths or between one and three minutes

Instructions:

1. Sit or stand upright, close your eyes, and bring attention to your breath. Become aware of the flow of your breath. Follow each breath as it flows in and out of your body. Be fully aware, awake, and present whilst breathing. Feel your entire body breathing.
2. If you like you can do a quick body scan, starting at the feet and moving gently upwards, until you reach the crown of your head. Be fully aware of the sensations present and of your body as a whole.
3. After three breaths, or if you have a minute, bring your attention back to your body. Become aware of your surroundings, open your eyes, and bring the meditation to a close. Return to your task rejuvenated.

> *Awareness alone exists.*
> *Prior to the arising of things.*
> *Awareness simply is.*
> *Upon the arising,*
> *Awareness is conscious of things,*
> *Things come,*
> *Things go.*
> *Birth, growth, dissolution.*
> *Amidst it all,*
> *Awareness is the unmovable;*
> *No where to go to,*
> *No where to come from.*

—Roy Melvyn, The Lost writings of Wu Hsin: Pointers to Non-duality in Five Volumes

Chapter 21
For Visualisation

Visualisation or visual imagination is a method often used in psychotherapy to practise a new behaviour or to alleviate stress. The visualisations described in the following meditations are metaphors for the activity of the mind. The MBSR programme uses metaphors of a lake and a mountain. The lake stands for a deep calm and stillness in its depths, untouched even when stormy winds rough up the surface and its waters become muddy, and the mountain stands for a still majesty, towering above us, unmoved by wind, weather, seasons, or calamities.

These meditations can be used when you are facing troubled times in your life. By embodying the lake, you can access the stillness deep inside you that is always unshakeably there.

LAKE MEDITATION

The visualisation of a lake is a particularly helpful form of meditation. Water has the power of receptivity. It opens for everything, only to close again, mirroring all that surrounds it, the surface sometimes muddy, sometimes crystal clear.

When: In moments of low self-esteem, when feeling emotionally low

Meditation posture: Seated or lying down

Duration: Ten to fifteen minutes

Instructions:

1. Sit comfortably, upright and relaxed, on a pillow or a chair or lie down on your back on a mat. Your arms must be at rest on either side of your body or folded in your lap. Close your eyes or, if uncomfortable, keep them half open, your gaze gently resting in front of you, preferably on the floor if seated. Breathe through your nose.
2. Once you have settled into your preferred posture, take four to five deep breaths. With each exhalation, relax the body and release any tense emotions, thoughts, or body sensations present. You can imagine sinking deeper and deeper into the mat or cushion, as if the earth is carrying you in her arms, caressing you, and holding you.
3. When you are ready, imagine a lake in front of your mind's eye. Your favourite lake, a pond, a surface of water surrounded by landscape, an alpine lake, or a lake from your imagination. A vessel filled with water held by the boundaries of rock and earth.
4. The surface of the lake mirrors its nature. The water is shades of blue or green, sometimes appearing deep or shallow, sometimes murky, or sometimes clear. When the wind is still, the surface is smooth like a mirror and reflects the surrounding trees, rocks, flowers, leaves, the sky, the clouds, the sun, the stars, or the moon. The

water, like a container, holds everything that is reflected in it from moment to moment.

5. Keeping this image of the lake, allow yourself to merge with the lake. Let yourself be held by awareness, with openness, and self-compassion just as the water of the lake is accepted and held by the earth.

6. Breathe with the image of the lake moment by moment. Feel its body as your body. Allow yourself to be open with your mind and heart, receptive to all that arises. Experience the moments of total silence when the water and reflected images are completely clear and other moments when the surface is restless, moving, agitated . . . and the reflections are lost for a while in the depths of the lake.

7. Observe the play of energy of your mind and heart—the fleeting thoughts and feelings, impulses, and reactions that come and go like waves. Recognise the effects in awareness that is similar to the ever-changing energies on the surface of the lake such as the wind, the waves, the light, the reflections, or the play of colours . . .

> Is the surface of your mind disturbed by thoughts or emotions? Can you recognise the waves as a familiar, essential aspect of a lake? Having a surface? Can you identify not only with the surface but also with the entire body of water so that you become like the stillness underneath the surface . . . steady and calm? Similarly, in your meditation practice and in daily life, can you identify with the vast,

steadfast reservoir of awareness that lies beneath the surface of the mind?

In the lake meditation, we sit with the intention to hold all qualities of the body and mind with acceptance, just as the lake is held by the earth. It is accepted and taken by the landscape, the moon, the sun, the stars, the trees, rocks, clouds, the sky, reflecting light. Just how the lake is caressed by the air and the wind, emphasising and underlining its essence, its vibrancy, and its inner glow.

(Source: Based on and adapted from Jon Kabat-Zinn, 'Lake Meditation', MBSR)

Sorrow prepares you for joy. It violently sweeps everything out of your house, so that new joy can find space to enter. It shakes the yellow leaves from the bough of your heart, so that fresh, green leaves can grow in their place. It pulls up the rotten roots, so that new roots hidden beneath have room to grow. Whatever sorrow shakes from your heart, far better things will take their place.

—*Rumi*

Chapter 22
For Gratitude

All religious traditions including Judaism, Christianity, Islam, Buddhism, and Hinduism encourage cultivating gratitude as an important moral virtue. For millennia, gratitude has been a popular topic among philosophers. According to Cicero, gratitude is more than 'the greatest virtue,' it is also 'the mother of all other remaining virtues.'

In many respects, research supports this sentiment. The experience of gratitude encourages us to appreciate what is good in our lives and compels us to pay this goodness forward. People with more grateful dispositions report being happier and more satisfied with their lives. Gratitude also functions as a social glue that nurtures the formation of new friendships, enriches our existing relationships, and motivates the very foundation of human society.

Practicing gratitude allows us to experience positive emotions and feelings for gestures and acts that we have encountered or are yet to encounter. Gratitude practice is also known to broaden our awareness and creativity and make us more successful in whatever we do.

Brother David Steindl-Rast, Austrian Benedictine monk and Zen practitioner, once said: 'It is not happiness that makes us grateful. It is gratitude that makes us happy.'

GRATITUDE MEDITATION

When: To evoke a positive mood through positive emotions, to promote hope, and when concluding your day

Meditation posture: Seated

Duration: Ten minutes

Instructions:

1. Sit comfortably in an upright position with your feet firmly on the ground, your shoulders, neck, and arms relaxed and your head straight. Allow your eyes to close or keep them gently focused in front of you.
2. When you feel you are grounded and have arrived in your position, take a minute or two to scan your body for any tension or tightness present. Release this tension as you exhale, letting it go. Similarly observe any emotions or troubling thoughts in your mind. Allow them to leave your system, releasing them consciously on the outbreath.
3. Now bring your awareness to your breathing, feeling your breath as it enters the body on the inhale and exits on the exhale. Breath by breath. Riding on the waves of the breath as the air gently moves in through your nostrils, your neck, your ribcage . . . raising your diaphragm and your abdomen when you breathe in . . . and makes its way out on the exhale, causing the belly to sink, the diaphragm to fall, and the chest to relax. Become one with the breath.
4. Gratitude can open the heart. You can also

accompany this meditation by repeating 'I am' whilst inhaling and 'grateful' whilst exhaling.

5. You may like to put a hand on your heart and say 'I am' as you breathe in and 'grateful' as you breathe out.
6. Bring to mind the things and people for which and to whom you are truly grateful and would like to express the same. You use the following words if you like:

> I am grateful for my family and loved ones.
>
> I am grateful for my friends, people who are here for me, lend me an ear, and support me when I need help.
>
> I am grateful for my health and quality of life.
>
> I am grateful to my teachers and the wisdom I have been able to learn from them.
>
> I am grateful to my parents and ancestors for enabling me to live as I do.
>
> I am grateful for my body and that I can see, hear, taste, feel, and walk.
>
> I am grateful for experiences in nature, a hike, the warm rays of the sun, and the air that I breathe.
>
> I am grateful to our planet earth for the food, the environment, the people, and animals that enrich my life every day.
>
> I am grateful for today and for this moment.
>
> I am grateful for life.

7. Remain in this inner awareness of gratitude and observe the sensations in your body and heart. How is your heart space now? Wide and open, warm and spacious? Perhaps you can now recognise that you can be grateful for your life, for the gift of life, and for the gift that you yourself are.
8. The feeling of gratitude may be permeating your entire body. Observe whether you can feel contentment, joy, and respect. Allow yourself to linger in the feelings that are arising.
9. Gently bring your attention back to observing your breath and become aware of the movement of the body during each breath.
10. Before you bring this meditation to a close, remind yourself to remain present and awake for every possibility to express gratitude. Slowly bring your attention back to the breath. Take three long and deep breaths, open your eyes, and end this gratitude meditation with a feeling of warmth in your heart.

(Source: Adapted from Mag. Klaus Kirchmayr, Geistreich and the gratitude meditation in the Mindfulness Based Compassionate Living Handbook)

Lord, make me an instrument of your peace.
Where there is hatred, let me sow love;
where there is injury, pardon;
where there is doubt, faith;
where there is despair, hope;
where there is darkness, light;
and where there is sadness, joy.
O Divine Master, grant that I may not so much seek
to be consoled as to console;
to be understood as to understand;
to be loved as to love.
For it is in giving that we receive;
it is in pardoning that we are pardoned;
and it is in dying that we are born to eternal life.

—St Francis of Assisi

Chapter 23
For Just Sitting

A meditation that requires you to simply sit is called the 'zazen' meditation. It is practiced in Japanese Zen Buddhism. Zen is the Buddhist tradition that developed from the Chinese school of Chan, which later spread to eastern Asia from India. It discarded the elaborate images and doctrines of *Mahayana* (also Tibetan Vajrayana) and took on fragments of Confucianism, Taoism, and Chinese culture. In Japan, Zen was further altered by absorbing, to some extent, the local Shinto cult.

In Zen there is no goal, but it teaches the direct contact with the soul. Moreover, instead of using lengthy discussions, paradoxes or *koans*[4] are often used to move from thinking to knowing. The discipline of Zen can seem extremely strict, but discipline is an important part of preparation for the spiritual path.

A few more words about koans or riddles, a practice used predominantly in the Rinzai school. The koan is like a mantra in yoga. It is an extreme and engaging method to force intense concentration on one single thought. In the Rinzai school, the master gives the student a personal koan, who may spend years trying to solve one before proceeding to another. The answer to a koan is not logically deducible by rational thinking and is not always verbal. Because the student must discard all thoughts, verbal associations, and any preconceived notions. The koan is a means of actively restructuring the ordinary linear mode of consciousness. Examples of well-known koans are:

> What is the sound of one hand clapping?
> What was your original face before you were born?
> Out of nowhere, the mind comes forth.
> Zen is a man hanging from a tree over a cliff. He is holding onto a twig with his teeth. His hands hold no branch. His feet can find no branch. Up on the edge of the cliff a man shouts at him: 'Why did Bodhidharma come from India into China?' If he fails to answer, he has lost. If he answers, he dies. What must he do?

There are different forms of Zen meditation. Artistic forms of Zen are the art of flower arrangement or Ikebana, the tea ceremony, painting, and calligraphy can also serve as meditation tools. Similarly, the martial arts are also part of Zen. Just as asanas and breathing exercises are a preparation for meditation, the martial arts such as judo, karate, aikido, kendo, iaido, and kyudo were originally practised to prepare the body and mind for zazen.

To be able to experience true Zen, the body must be put into a perfect state of balance and equilibrium so that its faultless functioning removes its very existence from the mind. The aim of Zazen is to establish harmony between the body, mind, and the breath in order to transcend them and maintain a state of *shunyata* or void where thoughts no longer arise. The mind is freed from all thought forms and is brought to a state of absolute emptiness.

When: For stillness of the mind
Meditation posture: Seated
Duration: Ten to thirty minutes or longer
Instructions:
1. Begin this meditation by taking a few deep, purifying breaths. Inhale gently through the nose and exhale through the mouth by forming a narrow oval. Repeat this three times.
2. Sit in an upright position in a chair or on a cushion. You can also face a plain wall, approximately a meter away. Keep your back straight and relax your shoulders and neck. Your eyes should be half open. Rest your gaze gently on the wall in front of you and relax your arms and cup your left hand in your right hand, with the tips of your thumbs gently touching each other—this is called the *dhyana mudra*.
3. Try and keep your body as still as possible during this meditation.
4. During this sitting practice, remain awake, alert, and present. Try not to focus or bring your attention to anything—not on any object, thought, image, sensation, feeling, or even your breath. Let the breath simply flow by itself in and out of the body.
5. Remain in this position for as long as you like.

The City of Brahman

In the city of Brahman is a secret dwelling, the lotus of the heart. Within this dwelling is a space, and within that space is the fulfilment of our desires. What is within that space should be longed for and realised.

As great as the infinite space beyond is the space within the lotus of the heart. Both heaven and earth are contained in that inner space, both fire and air, sun and moon, lightning and stars. Whether we know it in this world or do not, everything is contained in that inner space.

Those who depart from this world without knowing who they are or what they truly desire have no freedom here or hereafter. But those who leave here knowing who they are and what they truly desire have freedom everywhere, both in this world and in the next.

Like strangers in an unfamiliar country walking over hidden treasures, day by day we enter the world of Brahman while in deep sleep but never find it, carried away by what is false.

The Self is hidden in the lotus of the heart. Those who see themselves in all creatures go day by day into the world of Brahman hidden in the heart. Established in peace, they rise above body-consciousness to the supreme light of the Self. Immortal, free from fear, this Self is Brahman, the truth beyond the mortal and the immortal, he binds both worlds together. Those who know this live day after day in heaven in this very life.

The Self is a bulwark against the confounding of these worlds and a bridge between them. Day and night cannot cross that bridge, nor old age, death, grief, evil, or good deeds. All evils turn back there, unable to cross; evil comes not into this world of Brahman.

One who crosses by this bridge, therefore, if blind, is blind no more; if hurt, ceases to be hurt; if in sorrow, ceases to mourn. At this night itself becomes day; night comes not into the world of Brahman.

Only those who are pure and self-controlled can find this world of Brahman. That world is theirs alone. In that world, in all the worlds, they live in perfect freedom.

—*Chandogya Upanishad*

*Oh, Great Spirit,
whose voice I hear in the winds
and whose breath gives life to all the world, hear me.
I am small and weak.
I need your strength and wisdom.
Let me walk in beauty and make my eyes
ever behold the red and purple sunset.
Make my hands respect the things you have made
and my ears sharp to hear your voice.
Make me wise so that I may understand
the things you have taught my people.
Let me learn the lessons you have hidden
in every leaf and rock.
I seek strength, not to be superior to my brother,
but to fight my greatest enemy - myself.
Make me always ready to come to you
with clean hands and straight eyes,
so when life fades, as the fading sunset,
my spirit will come to you
without shame.*

—*Chief Yellow Lark*

Afterword

There is a space that I often point to in my meditation classes, a space in the middle of our chests. This is not a physical space, but a space of consciousness itself, the true presence of being. If you zone into your chest and listen very closely, with intuition, you may be able to feel a sense of warmth or expansiveness or perhaps something beyond sensation. You might like to put a hand there, or both, and abide for a while.

This space is our true home, a place outside of time and space that is always accessible and contains everything that exists. Here we can release everything—our body, our temporary role, our sense of I, me, and mine, our temporary identity, and become completely free.

The whole of life is in this empty heart space, not only us, as individuals, but the whole of creation, birth and death and life, joy and sorrow and whatever occurs on our life's journey from cradle to grave and in between. The heart space like a cosmic womb resonating with the primordial rhythm of the sound of existence. Throbbing, pulsating, vibrating, whilst everything constantly emerges and dissolves. Like the never-ending dance of the Indian god Shiva.

Here, the past, the present and the future exist simultaneously. All our memories, the memories of all things, everything we want to become and wish for, the fulfilment of all wishes, our entire life path is here in the space of the heart. All worlds, all sentient beings, nature, galaxies, universes exist side by side at the same time.

This inner place is bright, as if illuminated by thousands of suns. It houses the consciousness that reflects the inner and the outer.

The heart space is like a huge ocean and all universes and worlds are like the waves. We live in the foam of a wave, trapped in the dream of worldly existence. Shaken by happiness and suffering, joy and pain, transience, longing, having and rejection, until death catches up with us and we take on a new body. Because we are always focused on the external, distracted by the sense world and desire, always striving, we never come to rest. The fear of losing our egos and becoming nobodies, pushes us to constantly fight to remain someone. The someone as an identity, a persona locked in the world of the mind and our emotions and the illusory world we create for ourselves. Thus falls the veil of ignorance and we lose sight of the inner space, remaining an externality, a body limited in time and space. We forget the real I. The I of unlimited possibilities.

The space of the heart is the seat of insight. When we sit in stillness, the temple or caverns of the heart open their rooms and reveal their secrets, the secrets of wisdom, connection, and the universality of Being. Withdrawing from external and internal distractions, we sink into the inner heart space and lose ourselves, like a silent drop in the ocean of timeless and spaceless existence. By falling deep within ourselves, we merge with the innermost vastness of our Being, beyond life and death, ever there changeless.

Fixed as we are in the expression of form, we have forgotten the formless world, in which we also exist. The human and the grain of sand or stardust are ALL IS

Nothing manifests without preference for the one or the other. The grain of sand or stardust are also unlimited and omnipresent and follow the universal law, no coming, no going, only conversion of energy. It is only in the world of time and form that we notice differences. In that we value them, we confine ourselves to the form world. The formless world reveals itself in the heart space.

In the unlimited space of the heart lies your personal answer to humanity's greatest questions: 'Who am I? What is life? Is there a purpose in life? Why do we live?'

*Golden heart, silver heart, copper heart, iron heart . . . .
Is there anything that can be compared with the heart?
It dies and lives again; it is torn and mended again; it is
broken and made whole; it can rise and fall, and after
falling it can rise again instantly. It is a maze we enter and
when we are inside we can never get out. The heart can be
confusion and it can be paradise, it can be heaven itself;
and if we ask where we can see the soul manifest to view, it
is in the heart. What is paradise, where is heaven, where is
love, and where is God?*

—*The Heart by Hazrat Inayat Khan*

Author's Note

This compact handbook brings together inspirations, instructions and insights from different wisdom traditions that have been put together over the course of my years as a mindfulness and meditation teacher.

You can read this book from cover to cover or open it at a specific page or let a random quotation reveal itself to you. Apply the insights about self-management, create a stable relationship with your body, observe how the emotional tone develops, and be aware that thoughts are not facts. Feel emotions as they arise. Recognise what is emerging in you and around you from moment to moment, without succumbing to old patterns of judgment, naming, anticipation, bias, rejection, but simply being with whatever arises before a thought carousel begins.

Try the meditations that resonate with you, listen to the instructions if you would rather be guided (guided meditations can be downloaded for free from my website: www.esberger-mindfulness.com), or implement some or the other tip to live your life more mindfully. Perhaps some suggestions will be helpful for the troubled times we are living in.

Moving forward, it is your choice how you want to live your life from moment to moment, how you shape your own life, and how you shape your relationship with others. Beneath it all is what I have spoken of in the heart space, the awareness that is inherent in each of us. And that brings us to the fact that we are all intertwined and interdependent. All with everyone and everything in this universe. Like the stardust or the breath.

Perhaps the most important and profound thing is to continue our external life in 'doing' mode and at the same time to linger inside in 'being' mode. The balance of these two states reveals insights into 'not doing' and letting be done. To live every moment in its perfection because life is a chain of moments outside of time, form, and space. We create a fulfilling future when we are present, awake, curious, and attentive in these moments of here and now.

By living mindfully and heartfully in our own micro cosmos, we influence the larger macro cosmos around us. Small actions can transform the world and shape the evolution of our planet, for our children and our children's children, and the generations to come.

I would like to conclude with the words of Jon Kabat-Zinn from *Full Catastrophe* Living, 'Finally, just sit, just breathe, just rest in being present, being aware. And if you feel like it, allow yourself to smile inwardly, just a tad.'

May your mindfulness practice grow and flourish, nourishing and enriching your life, relationships, work, and health from moment to moment.

May you never forget what is inherent in you and that it may flourish!

Om Asato Maa Sad Gamaya
Tamaso Maa Jyotir Gamaya
Mrtyor Maa Amrtam Gamaya
Om Shaanti Shaanti Shaanti

[Lead me from non-existence, non-reality and untruth to existence, reality, and truth.
Lead me from darkness to light.
Lead me from death to immortality
Om Peace, Peace, Peace]

—**Brihadaranyaka Upanishad**

Acknowledgements

A deep bow of gratitude to all my respected teachers, noble friends, and students whose wisdom contributed to the germination of this book.

To my father, who started me on my journey home, who lost, won, and lost again, only to realise the unlosable.

To my mother, who taught me never to give up and to start over and over again regardless of the circumstances.

To my husband, Alfred, for accepting all my idiosyncrasies; and my son, Mathias, my silent guide.

To my sisters representing both intertwined realities in the now. Anu, who reconnected me. Nandita, in her pragmatism.

For the inspiration to delve into the world of mindfulness, my deep gratitude goes to Jon Kabat-Zinn whose books and training introduced me to an open form of meditation practice and brought me closer to Buddhism.

To the respected master Sri Mooji, who woke me up from sleep.

A deep acknowledgement to my first teacher, the renowned Swami Satyanandaji from the Bihar School of Yoga, who initiated me into this universe at a very young age.

The many masters and teachers who I have seen and heard along my life's path, Sri Krishnamurthi, Swami Chinmayananda, Swami Parthasarathy, Sri Poornananda

Tirtha, and Saki Santorelli to name a few. I owe you all deep gratitude.

My gratitude to my respected yoga teacher Sandeep Solanki, whose hatha yoga, pranayama, and meditation practice returned me to the source from which I had emerged.

Thank you, Susanna Kubelka, bestselling author, mentor, and guide to the world of writing, for inspiring me to put pen to paper.

Thank you, Payal Kumar, for believing in this manuscript and helping this book into print. My gratitude to Neha Chatwani for her advice and support in building bridges.

Thank you Friedhelm Boschert and Klaus Kirchmayr, noble friends on this journey in the now.

My gratitude to Jyotsna Nevatia for editing the first version of this manuscript and to Eberhard and Martina Nikitsch for their keen and expert input.

I would also like to thank and express my great appreciation to my editor, Sonali Pawar, from Hay House Publishers, India, whose interest, knowledge, expertise, and dedication moulded the manuscript into a book.

This book is dedicated to all, whose love and light I have encountered on my journey and to those who can benefit from one word, one movement, one space, or one breath.

Sarvesham Svastir-Bhavatu
Sarvesham Shantir-Bhavatu
Sarvesham Poornam-Bhavatu
Sarvesham Mangalam-Bhavatu
Om Shanti Shanti Shantih

[May there be an abundance of well-being in all,
May there be an abundance of peace in all,
May there be an abundance of fulfillment in all,
May there be an abundance of auspiciousness in all,
Om Peace! Peace! Peace!]

Bibliography

Alidina, Shamash. *Mindfulness for Dummies*. New Jersey: Wiley Publishing, 2011.

Analayo, Bhikkhu. *Satipatthana Meditation: A Practice Guide*. Cambridge, UK: WindhorsePublications, 2018.

Begley, Sharon. "The Brain: How the Brain Rewires Itself." *Time*, January 19, 2007. https://content.time.com/time/magazine/article/0,9171,1580438,00.html.

Bhikkhu, Thanissaro. 'Karaniya Metta Sutta: Good Will.' *Access to Insight*. 2004. http://www.accesstoinsight.org/tipitaka/kn/snp/snp.1.08.than.html.

Bhikkhu, Thanissaro. 'Sallatha Sutta: The Arrow.' *Access to Insight*, 1997. https://www.accesstoinsight.org/tipitaka/sn/sn36/sn36.006.than.html.

Bishop, Scott R., Mark Lau, Shauna Shapiro, Linda Carlson, Nicole D. Anderson, James Carmody, Zindel V. Segal et al. 'Mindfulness: A Proposed Operational Definition.' *Clinical Psychology: Science and Practice* 11, no. 3 (2004): 230–241. doi: 10.1093/clipsy.bph077.

Black, David S., and George M. Slavich. 'Mindfulness Meditation and the Immune System: A Systematic Review of Randomized Controlled Trials.' *Annals of the New York Academy of Sciences* 1373, no. 1 (June 2016): 13–24. doi: 10.1111/nyas.12998.

Bodhi, Bhikkhu. 'Toward a Threshold of Understanding.' *Access to Insight*. Accessed April 25, 2023. https://www.accesstoinsight.org/lib/authors/bodhi/bps-essay_30.html.

Brach, Tara. 'RAIN: A Practice of Radical Compassion.' *Tara Brach Blog*, January 1, 2020. https://www.tarabrach.com/rain-practice-radical-compassion/.

Brach, Tara. *Radical Acceptance: Embracing Your Life with the Heart of a Buddha*. New York: Bantam, 2004.

Braun, Ralf. *Mindful@Work, Anleitungen für eine achtsamen Arbeitsalltag*. Stuttgart: Klett-Cotta, 2018.

Brewer, Judson A., Patrick D. Worhunsky, Jeremy R. Gray, Yi-Yuan Tang, Jochen Weber, and Hedy Kober. 'Meditation Experience Is Associated with Differences in Default Mode Network Activity and Connectivity.' *Proceedings of the National Academy of Sciences* 108, no. 50 (December 2013): 20254–20259. doi: 10.1073/pnas.1112029108.

Brewer, Judson A., Sarah Mallik, Theresa A. Babuscio, Charla Nich, Hayley E. Johnson, Cameron M. Deleone, Candace A. Minnix-Cotton, Shannon A. Byrne et al. 'Mindfulness Training for Smoking Cessation: Results from a Randomized Controlled Trial.' *Drug and Alcohol Dependence* 119, no. 1–2 (December 2011): 72–80. doi: 10.1016/j.drugalcdep.2011.05.027.

Brook, Robert D., Lawrence J. Appel, Melvyn Rubenfire, Gbenga Ogedegbe, John D. Bisognano, William J. Elliott, Flavio D. Fuchs et al. 'Beyond Medications and Diet: Alternative Approaches to Lowering Blood Pressure: A Scientific Statement from the American Heart Association.' *Hypertension* 61, no. 6 (June 2013): 1360–1383. doi: 10.1161/HYP.0b013e318293645f.

Brown, Christopher A., and Anthony K. P. Jones. 'Psychological Correlates of Improved Mental Health in Patients with Musculoskeletal Pain after a Mindfulness-Based Pain Management Program.' *Clinical Journal of Pain* 29, no. 3 (March 2013): 233– 244. doi: 10.1097/AJP.0b013e31824c5d9f.

Brown, Kirk W., and Richard M. Ryan. 'The Benefits of Being Present: Mindfulness and its Role in Psychological Well-Being.' *Journal of Personality and Social Psychology* 84, no. 4 (April 2003): 822–848. doi: 10.1037/0022-3514.84.4.822.

Broyd, Samantha J., Charmaine Demanuele, Stefan Debener, Suzannah K. Helps Christopher J. James, and Edmund J. S. Sonuga-Barke. 'Default-mode Brain Dysfunction in Mental Disorders: A Systematic Review.' *Neuroscience & Biobehavioral Reviews* 33, no. 3 (March 2009): 279–296. doi: 10.1016/j.neubiorev.2008.09.002.

Buckner, Randy L., Jessica R. Andrews-Hanna, and Daniel L. Schacter. 'The Brain's Default Network: Anatomy, Function, and Relevance to Disease.' *Annals of the New York Academy of Sciences* 1124 (March 2008): 1–38. doi: 10.1196/annals.1440.011.

Burch, Vidyamala, and Danny Penman. *Mindfulness for Health: A Practical Guide to Relieving Pain, Reducing Stress and Restoring Wellbeing*, Piatkus, London: Piatkus, 2013.

Carim-Todd, Laura, Suzanne H. Mitchell, and Barry S. Oken. 'Mind-body Practices: An Alternative, Drug-free Treatment for Smoking Cessation? A Systematic Review of the Literature.' *Drug and Alcohol Dependence* 132, no. 3 (October 2013):399–410. doi: 10.1016/j.drugalcdep.2013.04.014.

Centers for Disease Control and Prevention. 'Adverse Childhood Experiences Reported by Adults—Five States, 2009.' Accessed April 25, 2023. https://www.cdc.gov/mmwr/preview/mmwrhtml/mm5949a1.htm

Chödrön, Pema *No Time to Lose: A Timely Guide to the Way of the Bodhisattva*, Colarado: Shambala Publications, 2005.

Cowen, Alan S., and Dacher Keltner. 'Self-report Captures 27 Distinct Categories of Emotion Bridged by Continuous Gradients.' *Proceedings of the National Academy of Sciences of the United States of America* 114, no. 38 (September 2017): E7900–E7909. doi: 10.1073/pnas.1702247114.

Davidson, Richard J. *The Emotional Life of Your Brain: How Its Unique Patterns Affect the Way You Think, Feel, and Live—and How You Can Change Them.* London: Hodder & Stoughten, 2012.

Davidson, Richard J., Jon Kabat-Zinn, Jessica Schumacher, Melissa Rosenkranz, Daniel Muller, Saki F. Santorelli, Ferris Urbanowski, Anne Harrington, Katherine Bonus, and John F. Sheridan. 'Alterations in Brain and Immune Function Produced by Mindfulness Meditation.2019 *Psychosomatic Medicine* 65, no. 4 (July–August 2003): 564–70. doi: 10.1097/01.psy.0000077505.67574.e3.

Desikachar, T. K. V. *Über Freiheit und Meditation: Das Yoga Sutra des Patanjali.* Germany: Via Nova, 2009.

Drath, Karsten. *Neuroleadership: Was Führungskräfte aus der Hirnforschung lernen können (Haufe Taschen Guide).* Germany: Haufe, 2017.

Duhigg, Charles. *The Power of Habit: Why We Do What We Do in Life and Business.* New York: Random House, 2013.

Dunlop, Julie. 'Meditation, Stress Relief, and Well-Being.' *Radiologic Technology* 86, no. 5 (May–June 2015): 535–55.

Epel, Elissa, Jennifer Daubenmaier, Judith T. Moskowitz, Susan Folkman, and Elizabeth Blackburn. 'Can Meditation Slow Rate of Cellular Aging? Cognitive Stress, Mindfulness, and Telomeres.' *Annals of the New York Academy of Sciences* 1172 (August 2009): 34–53. doi: 10.1111/j.1749-6632.2009.04414.x.

Farhi, Donna. *The Breathing Book: Good Health and Vitality through Essential Breath Work*. New York: Henry Holt, 1997.

Feldman, Christina, and Willem Kuyken. *Mindfulness: Ancient Wisdom Meets Modern Psychology*. New York: Guildford Press, 2019.

Feldman, Christina. *Boundless Heart: The Buddha's Path of Kindness, Compassion, Joy, and Equanimity*. Colorado: Shambala Publications, 2017.

Frawley, David. *Vedantic Meditation: Lighting the Flame of Awareness*. California: North Atlantic books, 2000.

Garrison, Kathleen A., Thomas A. Zeffiro, Dustin Scheinost, R. Todd Constable, Judson A. Brewer. 'Meditation Leads to Reduced Default Mode Network Activity Beyond an Active Task.' *Cognitive, Affective, & Behavioral Neuroscience* 15, no. 3 (September 2015): 712–720. doi: 10.3758/s13415-015-0358-3.

Gelles, David: *Mindful Work: How Meditation Is Changing Business from the Inside Out*. California: HarperOne, 2016.

Geurtzen, Naline, Ron H. J. Scholte, Rutger C. M. E. Engels, Yuli R. Tak, and Rinka M. P. van Zundert. 'Association Between Mindful Parenting and Adolescents' Internalizing Problems: Non-judgmental Acceptance of Parenting as Core Element.' *Journal of Child and Family Studies* 24, no. 4 (April 2015): 1117–1128. doi: 10.1007/s10826-014-9920-9.

Gilbert, Paul, 'Compassion: From its evolution to a Psychotherapy.' *Frontiers in Psychology* 11 (December 2020). doi: 10.3389/fpsyg.2020.586161.

Gilbert, Paul. *The Compassionate Mind*. London: Robinson, 2010.

Goenka, S. N. 'What Is Dhamma?' Vipassana Research Institute. Accessed 26 April 2023. https://www.vridhamma.org/What-is-Dhamma.

Goldstein, Carly M., Richard Josephson, Susan Xie, and Joel W. Hughes. 'Current Perspectives on the Use of Meditation to Reduce Blood Pressure.' *International Journal of Hypertension* (March 2012): 578397. doi: 10.1155/2012/578397.

Goldstein, Elisha, and Bob Stahl. *MBSR Every Day: Daily Practices from the Heart of Mindfulness-Based Stress Reduction*. California: New Harbinger, 2015.

Goldstein, Joseph. *Mindfulness: A Practical Guide to Awakening*. Colarado: Sounds True Publishing, 2013.

Goleman, Daniel, and Richard J. Davidson. *Altered Traits: Science Reveals How Meditation Changes Your Mind, Brain, and body.* New York: Avery Pubslishing, 2017.

Hansen, Rick. *Buddha's Brain: The Practicsl Neuroscience of Happiness, Love & Wisdom.* California: New Harbinger, 2009.

Hilton, Lara, Susanne Hempel, Brett A. Ewing, Eric Apaydin, Les Xenakis, Sydne Newberry, Ben Colaiaco et al. 'Mindfulness Meditation for Chronic Pain: Systematic Review and Meta-Analysis.' *Annals of Behavioral Medicine* 51, no. 2 (April 2017): 199–213. doi: 10.1007/s12160-016-9844-2.

Hoffman, Adam. 'How Mindfulness Improves Sleep.' *Greater Good Magazine*, October 19, 2015. https://greatergood.berkeley.edu/article/item/how_mindfulness_improves_sleep.

Hoge, Elisabeth A., Eric Bui, Mihriye Meta, Mary Ann Dutton, Amanda W. Baker, and Naomi M. Simon. 'Mindfulness-Based Stress Reduction vs Escitalopram for the Treatment of Adults with Anxiety Disorders: A Randomized Clinical Trial.' *JAMA Psychiatry* 80, no. 1 (January 2023): 13–21. doi: 10.1001/jamapsychiatry.2022.3679.

Hölzel, Britta K., Sara W. Lazar, Tim Gard, Zev Schuman-Olivier, David R. Vago, and Ulrich Ott. 'How Does Mindfulness Meditation Work? Proposing Mechanisms of Action from a Conceptual and Neural Perspective.' *Perspectives on Psychological Science* 6, no. 6 (November 2011): 537–559. doi: 10.1177/1745691611419671.

Hölzel, Britta, and Christine Brähler. *Achtsamkeit mitten im Leben. Anwendungsgebiete und wissenschaftliche Perspektiven.* München: O. W. Barth, 2015.

Hougaard, Rasmus, and Jacqueline Carter. *The Mind of the Leader. How to Lead Yourself, Your People, and Your Organisation for Extraordinary Results.* New York: Harvard Business Review Press, 2018.

Hülsheger, Ute R., Alina Feinholdt, and Annika Nübold. 'A Low-Dose Mindfulness Intervention and Recovery from Work: Effects on Psychological Detachment, Sleep Quality, and Sleep Duration.' *Journal of Occupational and Organizational Psychology* 88, no. 3 (March 2015). doi: 10.1111/joop.12115.

Hunter Emily M., and Cindy Wu. 'Give Me a Better Break: Choosing Workday Break Activities to Maximize Resource Recovery.' *Journal of Applied Psychology* 101, no. 2 (August 2015): 302–11. doi: 10.1037/apl0000045.

Jabr, Ferris. 'Cache Cab: Taxi Drivers' Brains Grow to Navigate London's Streets.' *Scientific American*, December 8, 2011. https://www.scientificamerican.com/article/london-taxi-memory/.

Kabat-Zinn, Jon, and Mark Williams. *Achtsamkeit: ihre Wurzeln, ihre Früchte*. Germany: Arbor, 2013.

Kabat-Zinn, Jon, Leslie Lipworth, R. Burncy, and W. Sellers. 'Four-Year Follow-up of a Meditation-based Program for the Self-Regulation of Chronic Pain: Treatment Outcomes and Compliance.' *Clinical Journal of Pain* 2 (1986), 159–774. doi:10.1097/00002508-198602030-00004

Kabat-Zinn, Jon. 'Some Reflections on the Origins of MBSR, Skillful Means, and the Trouble with Maps.' *Contemporary Buddhism* 12, no. 1 (June 2011): 281–306. doi: 10.1080/14639947.2011.564844.

Kabat-Zinn, Jon. *Coming to Our Senses: Healing Ourselves and the World through Mindfulness*. London: Piatkus, 2005.

Kabat-Zinn, Jon. *Full Catastrophe Living: Using the Wisdom of Your Body and Mind to Face Stress, Pain, and Illness*. New York: Delacorte, 1990.

Kabat-Zinn, Jon. *Wherever You Go, There You Are: Mindfulness Meditation in Everyday Life*. Hachette; 2005.

Kaluza, G. *Gelassen und sicher im Stress*. Berlin: Springer, 2007.

Keng, Shian-Ling, Moria J. Smoski, and Clive J. Robins. 'Effects of Mindfulness on Psychological Health: A Review of Empirical Studies.' *Clinical Psychology Review* 31, no. 6 (August 2011): 1041–1056. doi: 10.1016/j.cpr.2011.04.006.

Kerr, Catherine E., Stephanie R. Jones, Qian Wan, Dominique L. Pritchett, Rachel H. Wasserman, Anna Wexler, Joel J. Villanueva et al. 'Effects of Mindfulness Meditation Training on Anticipatory Alpha Modulation in Primary Somatosensory Cortex.' *Brain Research Bulletin* 85 no. 3–4 (May 2011): 96–103. doi: 10.1016/j.brainresbull.2011.03.026.

Killingsworth, Matthew A., and Daniel T. Gilbert. 'A Wandering Mind Is an Unhappy Mind.' *Science* 330, no. 6006 (November 2010): 932. doi: 10.1126/science.1192439.

Kim, Sooyeol, Seonghee Cho, and Youngah Park. 'Daily Microbreaks in a Self-Regulatory Resources Lens: Perceived Health Climate as a Contextual Moderator via Microbreak Autonomy.' *Journal of Applied Psychology* 107, no. 1 (March 2021): 60–77. doi: 10.1037/apl0000891.

Kohtes J. Paul, and Nadja Rosman. *Mit Achtsamkeit in Führung: Was Meditation für Unternehmen bringt. Grundlagen, wissenschaftliche Erkenntnisse, Best Practices*. Stuttgart: Klett-Cotta, 2014.

Kok, Bethany E., and Tania Singer. 'Phenomenological Fingerprints of Four Meditations: Differential State Changes in Affect, Mind-Wandering, Meta-Cognition and Interoception Before and After Daily Practice Across 9 Months of Training.' *Mindfulness* 8, no. 19 (August 2016): 218–231. doi: 10.1007/s12671-016-0594-9.

Kornfield, Jack. *A Path with Heart: A Guide through the Perils and Promises of Spiritual Life*, New York: Bantam books, 1993.

Kornfield, Jack. *The Wise Heart: A Guide to the Universal Teachings of Buddhist Psychology*. New York: Bantam, 2008.

Kuiken, Gerard D. C. *The Original Gita: Striving for Oneness*. Delhi: Motilal Banarsidass Publishers, 2015.

Langer, Ellen J. *Mindfulness*. Boston: Da Capo Press, 2014.

Langer, Ellen J., and Mihnea Moldoveanu. 'The Construct of Mindfulness.' *Journal of Social Issues* 56, no. 1 (January 2000): 1–9. doi: 10.1111/0022-4537.00148.

Lesser, Marc. *Seven Practices of a Mindful Leader: Lessons from Google and a Zen Monastery Kitchen*. California: San Francisco: New World Library, 2019.

Li, Wanqing, Xiaoqin Mai, and Chao Liu. 'The Default Mode Network and Social Understanding of Others: What Do Brain Connectivity Studies Tell Us.' *Frontiers in Human Neuroscience* 8 (February 2014): 74. doi: 10.3389/fnhum.2014.00074.

Löhmer, Cornelia, and Rüdiger Standhardt. *Timeout statt Burnout, Einübung in die Lebenskunst der Achtsamkeit*. Stuttgart: Klett-Cotta, 2012.

Luders, Eileen, Florian Kurth, Emeran A. Mayer, Arthur W. Toga, Katherine L. Narr, and Christian Gaser. 'The Unique Brain Anatomy of Meditation Practitioners: Alterations in Cortical Gyrification.' *Frontiers in Human Neuroscience* 6 (February 2012): 1–9. doi: 10.3389/fnhum.2012.00034.

Luders, Eileen. 'Exploring Age-Related Brain Degeneration in Meditation Practitioners.' *Annals of the New York Academy of Sciences* 1307 (January 2014): 82–88. doi: 10.1111/nyas.12217.

Lykins, Emily L. B., and Ruth Baer. 'Psychological Functioning in a Sample of Long-Term Practitioners of Mindfulness Meditation.' *Journal of Cognitive Psychotherapy* 23, no. 3 (August 2009): 226–241. doi: 10.1891/0889-8391.23.3.226.

Ma, S. Helen, and John D. Teasdale. 'Mindfulness-based Cognitive Therapy for Depression: Replication and Exploration of Differential Relapse Prevention Effects.' *Journal of Consulting and Clinical Psychology* 72 (2004): 31–40. doi: 10.1037/0022-006X.72.1.31.

Maehrlein, Katharina. *Erfolgreich führen mit Resilienz: Wie Sie sich und Ihre Mannschaft gelassen durch Druck und Krisen steuern*. Hessen: Gabal, 2015.

Maguire, Eleanor A., David G. Gadian, Ingrid S. Johnsrude, Catriona D. Good, John Ashburner, Richard S. J. Frackowiak, and Christopher D. Frith. 'Navigation-Related Structural Change in the Hippocampi of Taxi Drivers.' *Natl Acad Sci USA* 97, no.8 (April 2000): 4398–403. doi: 10.1073/pnas.070039597.

Marturano, Janice. *Find the Space to Lead: A Practical Guide to Mindful Leadership*. London: Bloomsbury, 2014.

Mascaro, Jennifer S., Marianne P. Florian, Marcia J. Ash, Patricia K. Palmer, Tyralynn Frazier, Paul Condon, and Charles Raison. 'Ways of Knowing Compassion: How Do We Come to Know, Understand, and Measure Compassion When We See It?' *Frontiers in Psychology* 11 (October 2020). doi: 10.3389/fpsyg.2020.547241.

Mindfulness All-Party Parliamentary Group. 'Mindful Nation UK Report.' October 2015. https://mindfulnessinschools.org/wp-content/uploads/2017/09/Mindfulness APPG-Report_Mindful-Nation-UK_Oct2015-1.pdf.

Mitchell, Jason P., Mahzarin R. Banaji, and C. Neil Macrae. 'The Link between Social Cognition and Self-Referential Thought in the Medial Prefrontal Cortex.' *Journal of Cognitive Neuroscience* 17, no. 8 (August 2005): 1306–1315. doi: 10.1162/0898929055002418.

Mukerjee, Radhakamal. *Astavakragita: The Song of the Self Supreme*. Delhi: Motilal Banarsidass, 2014.

Mulligan, Beth. *The Dharma of Modern Mindfulness: Discovering the Buddhist Teachings at the Heart of Mindfulness-Based Stress Reduction*. California: New Harbinger, 2018.

NICE Guidelines for Management of Depression. 'Depression in adults: recognition and management.' *NICE National Institute for Health and Care Excellence* (June 2022). https://www.nice.org.uk/guidance/ng222.

Notebaert, Karolien, and Peter Creutzfeld. *Wie das Gehirn Spitzenleistung bringt: Mehr Erfolg durch Achtsamkeit: Methoden und Beispiele für den Berufsalltag*. Germany: Frankfurter Allgemeine Buch, 2015.

Nummenmaa, Lauri, Enrico Glerean, Riitta Hari, and Jari K. Hietanen. 'Bodily Maps of Emotions.' *Proc Natl Acad Sci USA* 111, no. 2 (January 2014): 646–51. doi: 10.1073/pnas.1321664111.

Nyanaponika, Thera. (1962). *The Heart of Buddhist Meditation: A Handbook of Mental Training Based on the Buddha's Way of Mindfulness*. Massachusetts: Red Wheel/Weiser, 1994.

Nyanaponika, Thera. *Geistestraining durch Achtsamkeit: Die buddhistische Satipatthana Methode*. Germany: Beyerlein und Steinschulte, 1996.

Olszewska, Alicja M., Maciej Gaca, Aleksandra M. Herman, Katarzyna Jednoróg, and Artur Marchewka. 'How Musical Training Shapes the Adult Brain: Predispositions and Neuroplasticity.' *Frontiers in Neuroscience* 15 (March 2021). https://doi.org/10.3389/fnins.2021.630829.

Ortiz, Robin, and Erica M. Sibinga. 'The Role of Mindfulness in Reducing the Adverse Effects of Childhood Stress and Trauma.' *Children* 4, no. 3 (February 2017): 16. doi: 10.3390/children4030016.

Penman, Danny. 'The Three Minute Breathing Space Is Now Free to Download.' *Mindfulness: Finding Peace in a Frantic World*, July 28, 2011. http://franticworld.com/the-three-minute-breathing-space-meditation-is-now free-to-download/.

Romhardt, Kai. *Achtsam wirtschaften: Wegweiser für eine neue Art zu arbeiten, zu kaufen und zu leben*. Freiburg im Breisgau: Verlag Herder, 2017.

Rosenzweig, Steven, Jeffrey M. Greeson, Diane K. Reibel, Joshua S. Green, Samar A. Jasser, and Denise Beasley. 'Mindfulness-Based Stress Reduction for Chronic Pain Conditions: Variation in Treatment Outcomes and Role of Home Meditation Practice.' *Journal of Psychosomatic Research* 68, no. 1 (2010): 29–36. doi: 10.1016/j.jpsychores.2009.03.010.

Santorelli, Saki. *Zerbrochen und doch ganz: Die heilende Kraft der Achtsamkeit*. Translate by Ute Weber. Germany: Arbor, 2009.

Satchidananda, Swami. *The Yoga Sutras of Patanjali*. Virginia: Integral Yoga Publications, 1978.

Satyananda, Swami, and Satyananda Saraswati. *Asana, Pranayama, Mudra, Bandha*. Bihar: Yoga Publications Trust, 1997.

Satyananda, Swami, and Satyananda Saraswati. *Sure Ways to Self-Realization*. Bihar: Bihar School of Yoga, 2006.

Scharmer, Otto. *The Essentials of Theory U: Core Principles and Applications*. Oakland: Berrett-Koehler Publishers, 2018.

Segal, Zindel V., Peter Bieling, Trevor Young, Glenda MacQueen, Robert Cooke, Lawrence Martin, Richard Bloch, and Robert D. Levitan. 'Antidepressant Monotherapy vs Sequential Pharmacotherapy and Mindfulness-Based Cognitive Therapy, or Placebo, for relapse Prophylaxis in Recurrent Depression.' *Archives of General Psychiatry* 77, no. 12 (December 2010): 1256–1264. doi: 10.1001/archgenpsychiatry.2010.168.

Segal, Zindel V., J. Mark G. Williams, and John D. Teasdale. *Mindfulness-Based Cognitive Therapy for Depression: A New Approach to Preventing Relapse*. New York: Guildford Press, 2002.

Sheline, Yvette I., Deanna M. Barch, Joseph L. Price, Melissa M. Rundle, S. Neil Vaishnavi, Abraham Z. Snyder, Mark A. Mintun, Suzhi Wang, Rebecca S. Coalson, and Marcus E. Raichle. 'The default mode network and self-referential processes in depression.' *Proceedings of the National Academy of Sciences* 106, no. 6 (February 2009 2009): 1942–1947. doi: 10.1073/pnas.0812686106.

Siepmann, Anja. *Gelassen arbeiten: Wie Achtsamkeit den Berufsalltag erleichtert*. München: Scorpio, 2016.

Simons, Daniel J. and Christopher F. Chabris. 'Gorillas in Our Midst: Sustained Inattentional Blindness for Dynamic Events.' *Perception* 28, no. 9 (September 1999): 1059–1074. doi: org/10.1068/p28105.

Singer, Tania, and Matthieu Ricard. *Mitgefühl in der Wirtschaft, Ein bahnbrechende Forschungsbericht*. Translated by Michael Wallossek. München: Albrecht Knaus, 2015.

Steiner, André Daiyu. *Business Zen: Mit Achtsamkeit zu mehr Gelassenheit in der Führung*. New Jersey: Weinheim-Wiley, 2016.

Sternberg, Esther M. *The Balance Within: The Science Connecting Health and Emotions*. New York: Times Books, 2001.

Stocker, Christian, Jana Willms, Frtis Koster, and Erik van den Brink. *Mitgefühl üben: Das große Praxisbuch*. Mindfulness-Based Compassionate Living (MBCL). Berlin: Springer Wiesbaden, 2020.

Sze, Jocelyn A., Anett Gyurak, Joyce W. Yuan, and Robert W. Levenson. 'Coherence Between Emotional Experience and Physiology: Does Body Awareness Training Have an Impact?' *Emotion* 10, no. 6 (December 2010): 803–814. doi: 10.1037/a0020146.

Tan, Chade-Meng, Daniel Goleman, and Jon Kabat-Zinn. *Search Inside Yourself: The Unexpected Path to Acheving Success, Happiness (and World Peace)* San Francisco: HarperOne, 2014.

Tan, Chade-Meng. *Joy on Demand: The Art of Discovering the Happiness Within*. San Francisco: HarperOne, 2017.

Tang, Yi Yuan, and Michael I. Posner. 'Tools of the Trade: Theory and Method in Mindfulness Neuroscience.' *Social Cognitive and Affective Neuroscience* 8, no. 1 (January 2013): 118–120. doi: 10.1093/scan/nss112.

Taylor, Jill Bolte. *My Stroke of Insight: A Brain Scientist's Personal Journey*. London: Hodder & Stoughton, 2009.

Thera, Soma. 'The Way of Mindfulness: The Satipatthana Sutta and Its Commentary.' *Access to Insight*, 30 November 2013. http://www.accesstoinsight.org/lib/authors/soma/wayof.html.

Thich Nhat Hanh. *Happiness: Essential Mindfulness Practices*. Sydney, Australia: ReadHowYouWant, 2009.

Thich Nhat Hanh. *Miracle of Mindfulness: An Introduction to the Practice of Meditation*. Boston: Beacon Press, 1999.

Thich Nhat Hanh. *Understanding our Mind*. Berkeley: Parallax Press, 2002.

Treleaven, David, and Willoughby Britton. *Trauma-Sensitive Mindfulness: Practices for Safe and Transformative Healing*. New York: W. W: Norton & Company, 2018.

Vago David R., and David A. Silbersweig. 'Self-Awareness, Self-Regulation, and Self Transcendence (S-ART): A Framework for Understanding the Neurobiological Mechanisms of Mindfulness.' *Frontiers in Human Neuroscience* 6 (October 2012): 296. doi: 10.3389/fnhum.2012.00296.

van den Brink, Eric, and Frits Koster. *Mindfulness-Based Compassionate Living: A New Training Programme to Deepen Mindfulness with Heartfulness.* Oxfordshire, England: Routledge, 2015.

Wallace, B. Alan. *Buddhism with an Attitude: The Tibetan Seven-Point Mind Training.* New York: Snow Lion, 2001.

Wallace, B. Alan. *Minding Closely: The Four Applications of Mindfulness.* New York: Snow Lion, 2011.

Wallace, B. Alan. *The Four Immeasurables: Practices to Open the Heart.* New York: Snow Lion, 2010.

Weinstein, Netta, Kirk W. Brown, Richard M. Ryan. 'A Multi-Method Examination of The Effects of Mindfulness on Stress Attribution, Coping, and Emotional Well-Being.' *Journal of Research in Personality* 43, no. 3 (June 2009): 374–385. doi: 10.1016/j.jrp.2008.12.008.

Worline, Monica C., and Jane E. Dutton. *Awakening Compassion at Work: The Quiet Power that Elevates People and Organizations.* Pakland: Berrett-Koehler, 2017.

Notes and References

1. Bardo is the state of existence intermediate between two lives on earth according to some schools of Buddhism.
2. Samsara is Sanskrit for wandering or world.
3. Prosocial behavior benefits other people or society as a whole, such as helping, sharing, donating, co-operating, and volunteering.
4. A koan is a story, dialogue, question, or statement that is used in Zen practice to provoke the great 'doubt' and to practice or test a student's progress in Zen.